# sailing style

nautical inspirations for the home

## tricia foley

photographs by michael skott   text by jill kirchner simpson

Clarkson Potter/Publishers
New York

Published by Clarkson Potter/Publishers,
New York, New York
Member of the Crown Publishing Group,
a division of Random House, Inc.
www.randomhouse.com

CLARKSON N. POTTER is a trademark and POTTER and
colophon are registered trademarks of Random House, Inc.

Printed in China

Design by Richard Ferretti

Library of Congress Cataloging-in-Publication Data
Foley, Tricia.
    Sailing style: nautical inspirations for the home /
Tricia Foley; photographs by Michael Skott; text by
Jill Kirchner Simpson—1st ed.
Includes bibliographical references and index.
    1. Interior decoration accessories.    2. Ship decoration.
3. Nautical paraphernalia.    4. Seafaring life.    I. Kirchner
Simpson, Jill.    II. Title.
    NK2115.5.A25  F65    2003
    747—dc21                                    2002012219

ISBN 0-609-61026-0

10   9   8   7   6   5   4   3   2   1

First Edition

There is a poetry of sailing as old as the world.

—Antoine de Saint-Exupéry

# preface

Growing up on Long Island as the eldest of seven children, some of my fondest memories are of spending summer weekends on our old wooden boat, *Easy Living*. Of course there was nothing easy about it. When spring came, our Saturday-morning ritual became taking the canvas wrappings off the boat, scraping the barnacles from the hull, and scrubbing down the decks. Even the littlest child had a job to make it shipshape and seaworthy for the season. Old Maxwell House coffee cans were collected to bail out water, towels for the beach were rolled up to stash in the head, and ropes were coiled on elbows to be ready to tie up at the dock. While the boys were given lessons in tinkering with the mysteries of the ancient inboard motor by my father, the girls were hanging life preservers on the clothesline to air, and my mother was sewing up new navy canvas cushions for the bunks in the cabin below. Sailor hats and sneakers, duffel bags, and fishing rods came tumbling out of closets, and we were off to the boat club in our town to moor the boat for the season. We had an old Willy's Jeep and we all piled in on laps in our bathing suits and T-shirts with the dinghy tied to the roof. We would spend endless hours putting around Long Island Sound, anchoring at remote beaches, or meeting up with friends and family at the "West Bar" to tie up our little home on the water for picnics, shell collecting, and swimming.

Although I've lived in New York City for many years, and those lazy days of summer are long gone, it all comes back to me as soon as I'm near the water. Our family no longer has *Easy Living,* and the tide chart is no longer in pride of place on the refrigerator, but my father still goes down to the bluff every morning to check on the water and meet up with his old cronies and still knows when it's high tide and when "the blues are running."

I thought about those days often as we drove and sailed along the New England coast last summer and autumn in search of lighthouses and boathouses and cottages by the sea. As we looked for images that showed how nautical rituals and traditions have influenced home design, I realized that it was in my own home growing up that it all began for me. What I learned was not just about design and the aesthetics of the sailing tradition, but that respect for the sea and its environment, the manners of acknowledging and helping fellow boaters, and that keeping a tight ship are all important lessons in life.

Tricia Foley

left to right: Tom, Dennis, and Michael

# introduction:
# the lure of the sea

I have a sort of sea-feeling here in the country, now that the ground is all covered with snow. I look out of my window in the morning when I rise, as I would out of a porthole of a ship in the Atlantic. My room seems a ship's cabin; and at night when I wake up and hear the wind shrieking, I almost fancy there is too much sail on the house, and I had better go on the roof and rig the chimney.

—Herman Melville, in a letter to Evert Duyckinck, quoted in *Herman Melville* by Willard Thorp

Perhaps there is no more romantic dream than that of life by the sea, no means of travel more awe-inspiring than the simple power of wind captured by sail, no pastime more steeped in heritage and lore than sailing. Sailing has always embodied the sense of freedom and escape signaled by the horizon-stretching sea, the thrill and adventure of pitting one's own wits against nature's raw power, and the simple, practical elegance that has characterized sailboat design for centuries. Though the materials and the silhouettes of boats may have evolved, in essence, very little about sailing has changed: In an age of jet travel, it is still about hoisting simple triangular sails on a hull to harness the wind for travel or speed.

Sailing has captured our imaginations and permeated our culture in so many ways, and for so many centuries, that we are often not even aware of its influence—from navy blazers and bell-bottoms to bunk beds and hammocks, from rituals such as happy hour and flying the colors to sayings such as "all hands on deck" and "take him down a peg." In the home, the appeal of crisp white bead-board paneling; rugged natural fibers such as hemp, jute, and canvas; and the sleek modern simplicity of nautical hardware such as

grommets and cleats all attest to its influence, as does the current passion for collecting sailboat models and pond yachts, black-and-white sailboat photography, and sailing memorabilia—reminders, perhaps, of a slower-paced age. The enduring affection for blue and white stripes and fisherman's sweaters, the adoption by "civilians" of CPO shirts and Top-Siders; and the status conferred by a yacht-club burgee on a polo shirt or "Nantucket reds" speak to its attraction as well. This rich brew of customs and traditions has been culled over centuries from all forms of sailing, whether on fishing boats or yachts, merchant ships, warships, or racing sloops.

The large clipper ships that ruled the waves for over five hundred years, culminating in the "golden age of sail" in the 19th century, traversed the oceans in pursuit of distant lands, the merchant trade, and whaling. These were massive vessels built with elaborate rigging and an orchestra of sails in order to weather journeys of sometimes several years' duration. Many of the oldest customs of the sea, from sea shanties and colorful slang to sailors' striped jerseys, and the basic palette of materials from which most ships derived—canvas sails, wooden hulls, hemp ropes sealed with pitch, brass and iron fittings—date back to this era. Legend has it that Columbus discovered not only America, but also hammocks in the West Indies, and quickly adapted these for his crew to sleep in below deck. The development of increasingly sophisticated navigational instruments such as compasses, sextants, and chronometers paralleled the explosion in scientific discoveries and invention in this period, and these instruments have become highly sought-after collectibles today, as has the folk art, such as scrimshaw and ship's models, created by sailors to occupy their idle hours.

From Britain's Royal Navy and the United States Navy came the sense of formality, fraternity, tradition, and duty that we associate with sailing (and which are still carried forth by yacht clubs). Uniforms, from middy blouses to brass-buttoned navy blazers, ignited a passion for naval-inspired attire in Queen Victoria's time as well as our own. Traditions such as keeping time by the bells that sounded each half hour of a sailor's four-hour watch (so that 4 P.M. became "eight bells"—or in current parlance, time for drinks), keeping the ship's log (originally a method for measuring a ship's speed by timing the passage of a weighted wooden float, or log), and the precise sequence for flying the colors, or flags, of the ship and its country, were codified in the precise rhythms of life aboard ship in the navy.

In the 19th century, as Europeans and Americans began to have the means and leisure to pursue sailing not just for duty or work, but for pleasure and competition, the rarefied sport of yachting emerged. The sleek wooden boats designed for racing (some of which evolved from such workaday craft as single-masted catboats), came to epitomize the beauty and purist functionality that we most admire in classic sailboats today. Designed at the end of the 19th and the beginning of the 20th century by such legendary yacht designers as Nathanael Herreshoff in Rhode Island, Charles E. Nicholson in Britain, William Fife of Scotland, and Sparkman & Stephens in the United States, their sculptural forms in teak and mahogany, with flashes of brass and bronze, cutting through the water beneath billowing clouds of canvas, evoke all the beauty, glory, and bravura we associate with yachting at its finest. Many of these classic boats have been rescued and preserved, and continue to be sailed and raced today.

Sailboats, of course, have many similarities to houses, their snug cabins approximating the rooms of a home, from the galley (kitchen) to the saloon (living room) to the berths. And despite their limited size, or perhaps because of it, sailboats illustrate many of the features we appreciate most in design, and borrow for our homes, among them the careful economy of space, with no inch wasted and elements often doing double or triple duty; the crisp, elegant combination of highly varnished woodwork and light-reflecting white-painted planking; fitted furnishings that translate the comforts of home to the scale and stability appropriate for a boat, such as drop-leaf tables and banquettes, trim berths with drawers tucked beneath the beds; cabinets with caned doors for ventilation; and brass-rimmed porthole windows and skylights to invite in light and air.

Even today, on the simplest of daysailers, the neat serpentine coil of a line as it lays on the deck; the careful way every item is accounted for and neatly stowed, so it can be retrieved at a moment's notice; the simple, classic color scheme of white sails and perhaps a glossy midnight blue hull, accented with varnished wood trim; the attentive devotion to main-tenance; the elimination of all superfluous detail—all these elements attract us to the elegance of the sailboat. Its grace, its purity of form, its rigorous editing, chart the ways in which we might live simpler and more pleasing lives in our own homes.

*Sailing Style* examines the design legacy of the sailboat as inspiration for a clean-lined approach to modern living: its timeless palette of colors and materials, and its practical aesthetic; the architectural elements, both exterior and interior, that have been inspired by or adapted from nautical design; coastal architecture as defined by humble shipbuilders as well as grand Shingle Style architects; the instruments and accoutrements of sailing that have become not only valued collectibles, but touchstones for the bravery and beauty of a bygone age; and the romantic beacons that still have the power to lure us to the coast—lighthouses, boathouses, and sheltering harbors that offer safe ports in a storm. *Sailing Style* is an evocation of the ways in which homes by the sea—or those informed by the same relaxed, clean-lined sense of style—celebrate what is best about the boats that have set sail in our collective imagination for generations.

setting sail

A cloud of white canvas against a clear blue sky. The silvery gleam of cleats and blocks glinting in the sun. The smooth, glasslike surface of beautifully polished woodwork. Wood, cloth, rope—the simple, primitive materials used on boats for hundreds, in some cases thousands, of years, still evoke a

primal resonance for us. These classic elements—varnished mahogany set off by brass fittings, rugged coils of rope, the crisp, simple geometry of the sail plan—embody the beauty, purity, and simplicity that we associate with sailing. The icons that represent life by the sea have remained largely unchanged for generations: blue and white stripes, stitched white canvas, porthole windows, rope trim, anchors, the compass rose.

The elemental palette of colors and materials that has withstood the rigors of the sea points the way to an easygoing approach for decorating in the home: Dressed in the bleached grays of driftwood, the weathered whites of sailcloth, perhaps with touches of marine blue; enriched with the textures of hemp (which most ropes were once made of), sisal, and abaca; and polished with the gleam of dark woods such as mahogany and touches of silver or brass, a home can withstand the changes in fashion and trends as well as any properly reefed sailboat can endure a stormy sea. These natural colors and textures provide an ideal canvas, as it were, for more

personal elements, whether shells collected on the beach, photographs of favorite people and places, or treasures carried back from journeys abroad, just as clipper ship captains once did.

On boats, as in houses, it all starts with the materials: Early sails were first made of homespun wool, then linen and hemp, and finally cotton canvas, which was more taut and less porous. (In the inaugural America's Cup race of 1851, one of the reasons the America was able to defeat the Royal Yacht Squadron was because her sails were made of cotton, as opposed to the British boats' hemp.) Canvas was also used for sailors' duffel bags, ditty bags (small bags which held their tools), sometimes for hammocks, and also for decorative covers for seamen's chests. Canvas-covered cushions piped in a contrasting color (navy outlined in white, for example) have a nautical crispness, reminiscent of the cushions used for cockpit seating, banquettes, and berths. The canvas slings on BOC (British Officer's Club) chairs and some steamer chairs make them easy to fold and give them a maritime sensibility.

The wood used for building ships was chosen while it was still growing on the tree: An accomplished shipwright in the 18th and 19th centuries knew how to choose the right naturally curved boughs for the keel, or the ribs, and used the straight trunk for planking and decking. Sometimes saplings were even trained to grow into a desired shape. The wood, once harvested, was allowed to season and dry for a year, so that its natural warp could be taken into account as well. Each task was performed by carpenters who specialized in that particular trade, whether it be planking, caulking, joinery, or rigging. The wood most preferred for the keel was the sturdy elm; other parts might be made of red or white oak, pitch pine, or fir. England coveted the abundant forests of virgin timber in the Colonies to provide tall masts and ample lumber for her ships. (Any white pine larger than two feet in diameter was branded with the King's "broad arrow" and reserved as masts for the Royal Navy.)

The warmth of natural wood, its solid, substantial feel and beautiful graining, polished to perfection, are what makes it so appealing even today. On sailboats, the rich, deep coloration of varnished wood such as mahogany or cherry is often used effectively as a trim or contrast to white-painted walls, paneling, plank-

a wood staircase with white walls has the feel of a fine yacht's varnished brightwork, above left, a feeling reinforced by the primitive boat model on the landing. Left: A New England newel post wears a collection of weathered wooden buoys in a nod to its seaside setting.

23

ing, or beaded-board ceilings. The bright white surfaces bring a feeling of light and openness to below-deck quarters, where space and sunlight are limited commodities, while the wood trim provides rich detailing and definition.

On a ship, rope is literally the lifeline of the vessel: It forms the rigging that holds the sails aloft and allows them to be maneuvered; it might be the toe-hold or handhold that restores balance; it holds the anchor, secures the life raft, tows in the life-buoy. In the home, the natural rope fibers offer distinctive texture and tactile richness. Cord might be used as welting around pillows, upholstery, or placemats or for curtain tiebacks or shelf edging. It can serve, as it once did, as drawer pulls or handles on a chest. Rope carving may define a mantel, or a carved monkey's paw knot may serve as a curtain finial, for the quietest hint of nautical allusion. The appealingly rugged textures of sisal, jute, abaca, and hemp can also be seen in the woven rugs so popular today for the crisp neutral background they provide.

The simple, natural vocabulary of the sea offers a worthy compass for one's own home port, no matter the destination.

## old glory,
faded by the sun and misted by the fog, opposite, flies above a harborside house appropriately named "Float In," at the water's edge in Maine. Top right: The colorful graphic code of signal flags brightens the flagpole at The Charter Club on Cape Cod.

## flying colors

To communicate between ships at sea, navies developed their own unique sign language, using graphic code flags to send messages. The international code of signal flags comprises forty flags, including twenty-six alphabetical flags, ten numerical pennants, three substitutes (for repeat letters or numbers), and the code pennant. Each flag has a distinct meaning (for example, "F" means "I am disabled"), or they can be flown in various combinations for more elaborate communication. By the end of the 19th century, flag signaling had reached such levels of sophistication that there was supposedly a flag sequence for "May we borrow your first violinist?"

When a navy was victorious, its ships would sail into port with all their flags flying, hence the phrase "to come in with flying colors" ("colors" meaning the national flag). Today, on special occasions when yachts and ships "dress ship," the international code flags are hung from bow to stern in a magnificent display of pageantry.

# sailor stripes

Few elements are more instantly or universally recognizable as nautical icons than navy and white stripes. Perhaps at the most primal level, they evoke the line of the horizon, where sea meets sky, suggests the novelist Alison Lurie, although their affiliation with sailors and ships is a long one. Interestingly, the first horizontally striped tunics worn by sailors were probably red and white. English and Dutch paintings from the mid–17th century show sailors in such tunics, although the preference for blue and white soon predominated, and by the end of the 19th century, proliferated on shirts and even trousers, says Michael Pastoureau in *The Devil's Cloth,* a history of stripes. Boldly striped shirts—perhaps because they are more easily seen than solid colors —became the uniform of choice for the crew and deckhands, though not officers.

Antique and medieval sails were almost always striped, just as certain sails, such as spinnakers, continue to be. Signal flags and burgees were striped as well, further cementing the association between stripes and sailing. The stripes seen on sailing ships came ashore in the second half of the 19th century, as well-to-do Europeans discovered the pleasures of the beach and the exclusive sport of yachting.

Middy shirts and sailor suits, first worn by boys in training schools for the Royal Navy, then later by upper-class children on both sides of the Atlantic, also sported rows of thin stripes neatly outlining their cuffs and V-neck collars. In the late 19th century, women began wearing long full white linen dresses with middy collars and navy ties as well. Anything associated with the seaside, from cabanas and beach umbrellas to women's dresses and bathing suits, was almost always striped. Even men's jersey bathing costumes featured stripes, which were easy patterns to knit into simple garments.

In the late 1920s, Coco Chanel turned sailors' uniforms and yachtsmen's attire into the height of fashion, transforming men's tailored white flannel trousers, navy blazers, striped French sailors' jerseys,

vintage stripes of every dimension, united by their navy-and-white palette, create distinctive character in a beach house on Long Island, opposite. Overleaf: Light and airy blue-striped café curtains blow easily in the breeze. A white sailor's shirt hangs from the door.

shipshape

What is it about a boat? On deck there is the freedom of a boundless sea stretching to the horizon, the sense of exhilaration that comes from speed, from being out of doors, the bracing wind against one's cheek, the thrill of danger as the boat heels, whipping through the waves. Then down

below, an almost extreme contrast: the snugness, the rocking motion, the sense of protection that must recall for us, on some very primal level, the womb. It is these two distinct experiences of place and space that we often aspire to recapture in a home, particularly if it is one by the sea: the interaction with and openness to the outdoors (especially in good weather), along with the cozy, sheltering warmth of being safely harbored indoors (especially in stormy, raw, or chilly weather). During an age when so many seem to be building bigger and grander, it is important and reassuring to heed the lesson of the sailboat: that beauty can not only be found, but perhaps better appreciated, in small spaces; that greater satisfaction may be found in limitations and creative challenges rather than in an unending quest for "more."

Sailing has influenced architecture and design in wide-ranging and sometimes subtle ways. First, in the most basic sense, ship's carpenters often built houses as well as boats, and since ships were more difficult to design and construct, their craftsmen were especially skilled. After a joiner had framed and

built the house, a carver (who would have carved ships' figureheads) would come in to carve the moldings and ornamental details, such as fireplace mantels. For a ship's captain or owner, he might incorporate a scallop-shell motif or a carved-rope molding as a subtle allusion to the sea. On one fine Portsmouth, New Hampshire, house, for example, a carved whale-oil lamp motif crowns the pediments above the front door and the dormers, in a nod to the source of the original owner's fortune.

Some of the most direct correlations between ships and houses can be seen in longtime seafaring communities such as Nantucket. With space in these primitive houses at almost as much of a premium as on boats, people often slept in sleeping

sunlight streams through a window, opposite above, highlighting a ship's decanter, a model, and beaded-board paneling. A whitewashed anchor has found a new home port, below, nestled in a seaside garden on Cape Cod. Herbs such as lavender and scented thyme grow well by the sea, as do these hardy old-fashioned roses. A path of crushed shells leads to the house.

lofts, and the steep steps leading up to them were called escape scuttles because they were like the hatch (or scuttle) on a ship deck. In his White Pine Monograph of 1917, *Early Dwellings of Nantucket,* J. A. Schweinfurth notes, "There is a certain rule-of-thumb following of Greek precedent, influenced by hands and hearts which have builded [sic] many ships; a certain tightness, of shipshapeness; newel posts, rails, etc. suggest the crude but strong and rugged work of the ship's carpenter. They look as if they had weathered many a salty storm and stress, and yet inexpensive—there is no ostentatious display."

Cape Cod houses, both in the sense of the popular American house form as well as their place of origin, were built much like boats, with "a short hoist and a long peak," because they had to weather the same fierce nor'easters as ships on the Atlantic. One variation in the typical pitched and gabled roof of the Cape Cod house was the bowed or "ship's bottom" roof, which borrowed the same techniques used to build the hull of a ship. These houses might boast "ship's knees" (hefty angled braces) inside as well. Houses sometimes incorporated door frames, hatchways, cabinetry, and salvaged lumber from shipwrecks, which meant they were often slanted because they were literally "shipshape," built to fit the curved hull of a ship. The mortar used on chimneys was often made from mud and clamshells, while the plaster covering the interior walls was mixed from

# maritime memories

The tiny coastal communities along Buzzards Bay in Massachusetts as it wends its way to the Atlantic are generations-old sailing communities, not well-known in the way Nantucket, Martha's Vineyard, or Newport are, but familiar to any New England sailor worth his salt. Padanaram, Nonquit, Salter's Point, Round Hill—these are the picturesque enclaves that Bob Smith passes each time he takes a boat or ferry out to his family's summer home on the tiny island of Cuttyhunk (population: 125), in the Elizabeth Islands and once the home of many a whaling captain. Eleven miles or about forty-five stress-shedding minutes across Buzzards Bay, and he arrives at the claw-shaped harbor around which most of Cutty-hunk's homes are clustered, including his own.

Storms and hurricanes shape the coastline, the sailor's experience, and also the waterfront homes that sometimes have to weather the same extreme conditions as the boats. In the case of the Smiths' summer retreat, an unexpected hurricane in 1954 (see also page 126) washed away their house and everything in it. When they rebuilt the house, they moved it higher up the hill overlooking the bay, but it is still imbued with the past, thanks to sailing and fish-

ing mementos that aren't simply decorative collectibles, but rather personal items that pay tribute to Bob's father's prowess as a sailor and fisherman, and to the seagoing passions of a family.

The house is a simple, shingle-clad 1950s house, but it has been updated by whitewashing the paneling, adding Belgian linen and white cotton duck slipcovers and sisal rugs, and taking a modern, edited approach to sailing and fishing memorabilia. While most of the pieces in the house have a connection to family, friends, or the island, they have been used judiciously and displayed artistically, so that they don't overpower the space. The clean white

an antique standard from the Russian czar's royal yacht, opposite, is anchored on a picture rail by two black-and-white sailboat photographs, the one on the right being one of the great J boats that yachtsmen like J. P. Morgan and Thomas Lipton raced in what was then the World Cup, and became the America's Cup. Overleaf: A prize 142-pound tarpon caught in Key West presides over the guest bedroom, along with a pair of oars, an intricately hand-carved seaman's chest, and a watercolor of the family's first house that was lost to Hurricane Carol in 1954. The settee, covered in a tan-and-white Belgian linen stripe, chairs slipcased in the same fabric, and white seersucker bedspreads keep the mood light and summery.

# sailboat photography

One of the most appealing, affordable, and increasingly popular areas of collecting is black-and-white sailing photography, where good images can still be found at affordable prices. The higher end features such well-known maritime photographers as Beken of Cowes, a four-generation family firm (the best-known of whom was Frank), who have been photographing yachts and America's Cup races since 1888 in Cowes, on the Isle of Wight; and in the United States, Morris and Stanley Rosenfeld, another father-and-son team, whose extensive collection of marine photographs now belongs to the Mystic Seaport Museum. Other well-known 19th-century names include Nathaniel Stebbins, who photographed ships in Boston and New York, Edwin Levick, Henry Peabody, J. S. Johnson, James Burton, and C. E. Bolles.

As with other forms of fine art photography, the serious collector should buy original vintage prints, not reprints from old negatives. For more decorative purposes, affordable new prints and reproductions of classic images are readily available. There are also a number of talented contemporary photographers who specialize in sailboats.

and pale sea green rooms form a crisp backdrop for black-and-white photographs, exuberant stuffed trophy fish, beachcombed shells, and nautical charts and flags. Old comfortable family furnishings are dressed in summer whites, and spectacular views of the harbor are framed with sheer white curtains. As they added on to the three-bedroom house over the years, they took care to site each room to offer a scenic view of the boats bobbing in the water, their white masts and hulls sparkling against the sapphire sea. Visiting sailors overnighting in the guest room can check on their boats in the harbor from the comfort of their beds, and friends tend to linger over cocktails on the spacious deck as the sun sets.

Bob's father's deep connection to the sea, fostered since he was a boy, still lives on in sailing trophies and fishing reels, a salt-pitted compass and binoculars, and a sleek sailboat model he carved when young. The silver sailing trophy he won from the New Bedford Yacht Club on his Herreshoff yawl,

great catch. A trophy bass caught off Cuttyhunk in 1954, opposite above left, caps a row of fishing photographs. Above right: This antique leather-bound navigational book of New England includes fold-out charts printed on delicate rice paper as well as drawings of the rocky, treacherous coastline in profile to aid sailors. Not all that much has changed since the 1860s, when this book was published. Below left: This silver trophy pitcher was awarded in 1931 by the nearby New Bedford Yacht Club. The silver toast rack, below right, found at an antiques shop, sports a burgee from an unknown private yacht.

and furnishings of teak and painted wood designed to withstand heavy weather. Teak, which along with mahogany and cedar naturally resists rot and splintering, is so sturdy that it can survive even a shipwreck, as the steamer chair here actually did. It was salvaged from the Cuttyhunk shore, where it had washed up from the wreck of the *Andrea Doria* in 1956 off the coast of Nantucket.

Steamer chairs and deck chairs evolved from British campaign furnishings and their later, simpler incarnation, Edwardian camp furniture. The campaign chair, designed for British army officers in India, was made of oak legs and stretchers with a canvas seat and back and leather strap armrests. This became the folding deck chair so popular on boats and patios today for its casual, utilitarian comfort, as well as its portability and ease of storage. Wooden steamer chairs, originally designed for use on ocean liner decks, are yet another successful adaptation for modern outdoor living.

From the saillike slipcovers inside to the steamer chair outside, this is a house in which almost every element subtly celebrates its connection to the sea.

a stark souvenir of the sinking of the *Andrea Doria,* this teak steamer chair, opposite, which washed up on the Cuttyhunk beach along with life preservers and other flotsam, bears quiet witness on the deck, offering a front-row view of all the harborside comings and goings.

# the hammock

Beds on large whaling, merchant, and war ships were often simple rope or canvas hammocks. Legend has it that Columbus saw natives in San Salvador sleeping in cotton nets slung between trees and adopted the idea for use on vessels. They were originally used as litters, or stretchers, for the sick, but eventually came into wide use for sleeping—for example, in the Royal Navy, where two men often shared one hammock. They were especially useful on war ships, because the main gun deck (where the crew slept) had to be quickly cleared during battles.

There are a variety of different hammocks, many introduced by sailors, with perhaps the best-known being the Pawley's Island hammock. A South Carolina riverboat pilot is said to have created the first of these famous rope hammocks for sleeping on his boat on hot nights in the 1860s. The Gloucester hammock comes from the Massachusetts seafaring town of the same name, and is sewn from heavy cotton duck, like the sails of Gloucester schooners. It is more like a long upholstered porch swing.

Hammocks today are a well-loved symbol of relaxation: Strung between two trees or porch posts, they are an invitation to take a leisurely nap, with the breeze wafting through the open cotton or jute net, swaying the hammock like the rocking of a boat.

# a yacht not launched

On a pristine spot along the coast in Watch Hill, Rhode Island, with a picture-postcard view of the Watch Hill lighthouse and the sea, one boat-smitten homeowner has taken an almost literal approach to nautical style in his home and gatehouse. As the designer and builder says, "They are like yachts that were never launched."

With a succession of additions over the past century, the original 1914 house had lost its original character, so the new owner started from scratch, but with a determination to use the highest quality materials and an even better level of craftsmanship than had been bestowed on the original house. The gatehouse, which is now a one-bedroom guesthouse and garage, is a perfect study in how the trim, compact design of a boat can be the ideal template for making the most of every square inch in a small house. Like a fine yacht, this house was fitted with quality teak, cherry, and mahogany moldings and brightwork, all custom-made. It took the workmen months just to complete the sanding, and the woodwork was not polyurethaned, but varnished the old-fashioned way, with seven separate coats. (Brightwork refers to the highly varnished woodwork both above and below deck that is the pride of any classic boat owner. As the saying goes, "bright it should be, and work it is.")

The polished natural wood is tempered by lots of white—on painted beaded-board and paneled walls and shiplap ceilings throughout—so that the effect is bright and light, not dark and dreary. Rounded corners give the feel of a boat's pilothouse, while wood-paneled skylights in the ceilings offer a view to the sky, and wooden gratings covered by glass in the floor show through to the rooms below, just as they would in a boat.

Nearly all the furniture is built-in, from the twin beds and dresser drawers in the bedroom to the space-saving drop-leaf dining table and banquette,

## a compass rose, accurately pointing due
north, is inlaid in the heart pine floor of the entry to the guesthouse, opposite. Even though the first floor of the guesthouse contains just a garage and shower for beachgoers, it is lavished with the same five-foot-high paneled wainscoting, beaded-board walls, and shiplap ceilings, all painted white, as the rest of the house. The "V" pattern of the door was inspired by one seen in Switzerland. The distinctive brass hardware and lighting gleams just as it would on any well-maintained yacht.

to the windowed alcove, with its upholstered cushions piped in navy and white, which is designed to feel like the transom of a ship. Every nook and cranny is fitted with built-in drawers and storage or window seats, and skylights are carved out of many of the eaves as well. The skylights are mullioned, as they would have been in the late 19th century, and almost all the light fixtures are taken from ships or are replicas of those used for ships.

The diminutive kitchen, like a sailboat's compact galley, has a small-scale sink and appliances, copper counters, and wood cabinet doors grated for ventilation. The door adjacent to the "head" has a frosted porthole window whose curves are echoed in the door's rounded form. And just as a tiny slice of a gorgeous view can liberate the sometimes claustrophobic feeling below deck, a small window just above the sink rewards the dishwasher with a perfect view of the lighthouse and sea, while a skylight

## the graceful arch of the porte cochere,

opposite above, frames a perfect view of the Watch Hill lighthouse, which the owner graciously extends to passersby. The house is clad in red cedar shingles treated with a bleaching oil to turn them a uniform gray, though the cedar is left raw on the underside of the porte cochere roof to dramatic effect. The wooden floor of the drive-through gives the feeling of crossing over a wooden bridge to an island as you enter the property. In the main house, below, the same curve, but paneled, is echoed in the ceiling of the stairwell, with a skylight built into its arch. Overleaf: The window seat, with its piped cushions and varnished ship's "knees," feels like the transom of a ship. Beaded-board walls and built-in cupboards, as well as a pond yacht, extend the shipboard theme.

## ship's lanterns

The earliest ship's lanterns, from the beginning of the 18th century, used candles and were constructed of gilded wood lined with metal. By the 1820s, metal and glass lanterns were lit with whale oil, which gave better light. In the late 1850s, kerosene became widely available and lanterns began to be mass produced. Lanterns were generally made of copper and brass with thick-ribbed, curved glass lenses. Bull's-eye, convex, or Fresnel lenses (also used in lighthouses) were often molded into the glass helped to intensify or focus the light.

Inside ship cabins, oil lamps were mounted on gimbals (pivoting rings, used to keep them level as the ship rolled). Lanterns carried by those on watch had wire cross guards or cages to protect the glass globe.

Many designs are made as reproductions today, either as electrified lights, often for outdoor use, or as old-fashioned oil lamps. Antique lanterns in good condition can also be fitted with a new wick and globe and lighted with kerosene.

spills sunlight from above. The boating metaphor even extends quite literally to the entrance stairs, where a hatch can be slid across the opening to seal off the guest quarters from the entryway.

The remarkable achievement of the house is that it pays homage to the architecture and ornament of a sailboat without becoming a clichéd or overwrought re-creation of a ship. The balance of elements is the result of research at maritime museums like Mystic Seaport and inspiration culled from classic boat magazines and from beautiful boats themselves. The rest of the decoration is kept simple, so that the woodwork and architectural elements can stand out. The fabrics are limited to simple navy-and-white plaids, or solids piped in crisp contrasting outlines like boat cushions. There are no window treatments to obscure the stunning views and few rugs covering the antique heart pine floors. It's no wonder the guesthouse is even more coveted for overnight stays than the main house.

brightwork, polished to a shine, mixes with painted white beaded-board and paneling throughout, just as it did on the finest yachts. Opposite, clockwise from top left: In the guest bedroom, the bunks and cupboards are all built-in; the arched ceiling motif is repeated with a paneled skylight. Louvered doors and a sliding hatch cover provide a snug sense of privacy instead of a foreboding view down a long stair. Built-in window seats offer cozy spots for lounging or even sleeping; the curved railing frames the half-round skylight set into the eaves. A pair of highly varnished arched doors, flanking a classic brass sconce in the entry, could be mistaken for a yacht's interior.

## galleys

The extremely compact kitchens on boats can make any homeowner feel like a cook in a castle by comparison, and they are often filled with good space-saving ideas for any small kitchen. Some useful galley features:

· Appliances are often compact under-counter models; two-burner or three-burner cooktops can often suffice for most needs, and an oven might not be needed at all.

· Wooden cutting boards designed to be fitted over the sink and/or stove when not in use add bonus work space, as do slide-out or fold-up counter extensions.

· Cabinets often have sliding doors, so that they don't open into the space, and the doors may be louvered for circulation.

· Wineglasses are often stored upside down on hanging racks; plates and glasses stored in racks above the sink can drain in place.

· Narrow shelves or recessed compartments along the backsplash make use of wasted space.

· Bins to hold utensils can be sunk into a countertop or built into shelving, since galley drawers are often nonexistent.

marine blues

The endlessly varying, breathtaking blues of the sea and the sky are cooling, calming, refreshing. From the turquoise brightening the interior of a dinghy, below left, or a dock, bottom right, to the more grayed marine blues that work beautifully with weathered shingles, top left and bottom center, on Cape Cod, and below right, in Nantucket, true blues never go out of style. The color blue, etched in silhouettes of sailboats and lighthouses, on shutters and signs, or even on the binding of a book, left, instantly telegraphs the sea.

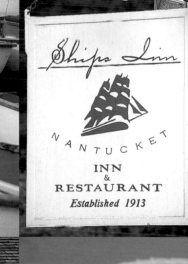

a seafaring
legacy

As children we may have marveled at the sound of the sea in a conch shell far from the shore, or the miracle of a fully rigged ship formed in perfect detail inside the confines of an old glass bottle. For collectors, the same sense of wonder is ignited by holding a brass spyglass or a well-worn wooden ship's wheel

once used by a famous captain; tracing the etched path of a scrimshaw engraving on an awe-inspiringly large sperm whale's tooth; or studying the symmetrical beauty of a nest of Nantucket lightship baskets woven by sailors whiling away the hours on coastal lightships.

These talismans of the sea also spark our intellectual curiosity and desire to understand and know history on a more personal scale. We may respond to the primitive, unselfconscious artistry of the sailor who, with hours of quiet time on his hands, patiently constructed an intricately detailed replica of his ship in a three-dimensional diorama. We can experience the vicarious thrill of the America's Cup race in one of the beautiful black-and-white photographs of sailboats and races taken by some of the sport's most respected artists. We can marvel at the feats of engineering and beauty in the wooden half models of the exquisitely designed yachts by the likes of Olin Stephens, Nathanael Herreshoff, and many others, or find a simple charm in the model boats that a homebound fisherman might have carved by the fire

during the off-season. Silver yachting trophies, old pennants and flags sewn from wool and mellowed by age, sand glasses and spyglasses, ship's bells and bo'sun's whistles, lighthouse lenses and ship's lanterns, seamen's chests with their braided rope beckets, porthole windows, and whaler's harpoons are just some of the many mementos of the sea that have become highly desirable collectibles.

One can inhabit even more fully the world of the whaler or the merchant seaman or the naval officer by reading his journal or a ship's log, penned in ink, perhaps even punctuated by watercolor sketches, or in the case of whaling logs, graphically stamped with silhouettes of whales caught or the flukes (tails) of the ones that got away. These windows onto another world, filled with the sometimes dramatic,

a clipper ship racing through the water, opposite, was captured in watercolor by a sailor named Noyes Lewis, who painted the many ships he had sailed on or observed in a remarkable sketchbook now in the collection of Ken Martin (see page 109 for more).

## nameboards

Carving was not only the sailor's pastime to relieve boredom during long winter's nights at home, but it was also a means by which owners and captains distinguished their vessels from other ships on the open seas. Figureheads and fancy embellishments in the captain's cabin might be examples of the carver's art on the finest ships, but even the humblest proudly bore their christened names on carved boards affixed to the stern.

When a ship docked in its home port, the captain often took the carved nameboard (also known as a sternboard) and hung it on his fence or house to announce that he was home. In time, houses began to be called by these names as well, like the centuries-old houses in 'Sconset, on Nantucket, with names such as "Don't Give Up the Ship," "Snug Harbor," "The Anchorage," and "In and Out."

Goldsworthy Dutton, as well as Currier & Ives, was being engraved on lithographs for sale to the general public. There were also sailors who painted ship portraits instead of whittling models in their leisure time.

By the end of the 19th century, photography began to take the place of painting. Photographers such as Alfred Beken in England and Morris Rosenfeld in New York became the new portraitists of sailing ships, particularly of racing yachts, an art form that continues to be especially popular today (see page 56).

All of these collectibles are often very much at home in houses by the sea, where a seascape painting reflects the view outside the window, and a mariner's old compass or telescope can still be used to explore the sea and its environs. Even as they seem to have found their bearings in such surroundings, they exert their spell of wanderlust and the resonance of history no matter where their location.

thar' she blows. An elaborate tin ship weathervane features intricate rigging and a pierced yacht ensign on this curvaceous Victorian cupola, opposite. A carved eagle signboard hangs beneath a porthole window on the clapboard siding.

# a beacon for collectors

It is hard to imagine a more picture-perfect setting for dealers in maritime antiques than a lighthouse. On the coast on Cape Cod's south shore, this picturesque whitewashed brick lighthouse and clapboard keeper's house, built in 1847, protected sailors from the rocky coastline from 1849 to 1929. Like many decommissioned lighthouses, it fell into great disrepair and was abandoned. When antiques dealers Alan Granby and Janice Hyland bought it in 1985, it took years of rebuilding to make it habitable again. In the process, they rebuilt the lens room (now a place for entertaining friends and reveling in the views of Nantucket Sound), and created a series of light-filled additions that showcase their fine maritime antiques.

The clean-lined, white-walled, and white-furnished rooms form a gallerylike backdrop for an impressive collection amassed over the past 25 years. The living room fireplace, for example, was sized and designed specifically to showcase two treasured pieces: an 1870s half model of an American coastal schooner and a late-18th-century sternboard carving of a war eagle clutching a cannonball, one of the oldest American sternboard carvings known to exist.

Though the living room and master bedroom are new additions, they feature exposed beams and rafters, custom-milled from fir and stained to look as if they are old, to form a fitting setting for the centuries-old collectibles, including a flotilla of 19th-century ship models that sail across the beams of the bedroom, so that they seem to float upon the sea outside when you are lying in bed looking up at them. And while the sofas and chairs are certainly comfortable and inviting, there is no question the space is as much art gallery as home—a showcase for prized acquisitions, from fine marine paintings by such masters as Robert Salmon, Fitz Hugh Lane, and

the lens room sports a copper roof, just one of many necessary renovations at this restored lighthouse home on Cape Cod, opposite. The large iron bell once rang from a Nantucket lightship. Overleaf: In the renovated living room, an English rope-carved yacht tiller with a ram's-head end, from the late 19th century, has pride of place hanging from a center beam. Some volumes from the extensive maritime library fill the bookshelves; the globe, dating from 1852, is the only known example of an American carved-pineapple base on a Copley globe (New York's earliest globe maker). Over the slant-top China Trade padauk wood desk in the center of the far wall is a rare Aaron Willard banjo clock with an alarm bell from about 1880.

the barometer (from about 1826) hanging on the galley wall, opposite, has a one-of-a-kind case, custom-made from 120 different bands of specimen woods, all identified on the back. It hangs above a Massachusetts Federal card table. The painting of the yacht Siren, by Conrad Freitag, dates from 1882; the writing-arm Windsor chair is by Wallace Nutting. The living room fireplace, above, was designed to showcase one of the oldest known American sternboard carvings, with exquisite detail, and a half model of an 1870s American coastal schooner. To the left of the fireplace is a collection of 19th-century American ship's clocks from such makers such as Boston, Howard, and Chelsea.

James Buttersworth, to ship models, scrimshaw and navigational instruments.

Many of the pieces displayed in this home are museum-quality, among the best of their kind in the world. There are many examples of fine carving, from what is arguably the best rope-carved English yacht tiller to an American eagle paddleboat carving. There is a tall clock by the most famous American clock-maker, Simon Willard, from 1805. Its original bill of sale makes it especially valuable, but it is the way the small ship rocks back and forth upon the sea on the face of the clock as it ticks that makes it so enchanting. There are gimbaled ship's barometers and antique globes, scrimshaw rolling pins and astronomical telescopes at every turn.

Connections to the sea run deep here: A sixth-order Fresnel lens, the type that would have been used in the original lighthouse, hangs from the rafters. The living room coffee table was made from a child's rowboat, and the kitchen counter is an 1860s marble oyster bar recycled from Janice's family's fish market. Even the newly added deck features a copper compass rose motif inset into the wood flooring.

Perhaps the most valuable collection in the house is a 2000-volume maritime library, one of the largest privately owned collections in the world. Filled with rare books dating back to the 1600s, its beautifully colored leatherbound volumes offer 400 years of sailing history, from the merchant marine to racing yachts, from naval architecture to yacht clubs.

# ship models

Ship models were made for a variety of purposes: Half block models (divided vertically down the center and usually mounted on wood plaques) were made by boatbuilders as aids in the design process, either as an intermediary stage between drawing and building, or as the plan itself.

Detailed full models of ships were often made as presentation models by builders for owners, for approval during the building process, or as a gift upon its completion. Shipbuilders might also make models for advertising at trade fairs or to commemorate important commissions. Equally elaborate are the prisoner-of-war models made from bones by Frenchmen captured by the British during the Napoleonic Wars, and the carved ivory ships made in Dieppe, usually only about three to five inches long and encased in glass domes.

Votive models, more crudely made and brightly painted, were made to be hung in churches in seaport and fishing communities in honor of a patron saint, such as Saint Nicholas or Saint Anthony, in gratitude for a safe and successful journey. Sailors also made models of the ships they served on for themselves or as gifts—everything from small ships inside bottles to dioramas and bas-relief picture models with carved wooden sails, mounted on putty or wooden seas against a painted sky, and set inside a picture frame or case.

# instrumental collections

One of the earliest navigational instruments developed, and still in use, is the compass. A compass takes its bearing by means of a magnet, which, aligned with the magnetic pull of the earth's metallic core, is able to determine due north. The compass rose, often lavishly illustrated on the compass card, illustrates the 32 points of direction, from north-northeast to south-southwest.

A procession of instruments were devised to help measure latitude, including the quadrant, the astrolabe, the cross-staff, the backstaff, the octant, and finally the sextant, which were increasingly refined attempts to help the mariner determine the angle between the sun at noon and the horizon, or the height of the polar star at night. (With the exception of the sextant and octant, many of these instruments are quite rare and usually seen only in museums.) With tables to correct for the time of year and the hemisphere, the sailor could then determine his latitude. Until a reliable method was devised for measuring longitude, sailors often sailed along lines of latitude.

It was understood as early as the 15th century that longitude could be determined by the difference between local time and Greenwich Mean Time. (One hour's difference in time is equal to 15 degrees of longitude.) But it was extremely difficult to devise a clock that would maintain the pinpoint accuracy required, with the variations in temperature, humidity, and vigorous movement on a ship. In 1714, the British government offered a prize of £20,000 to the person who could invent a method for doing so accurately. It took until 1759, when a humble clock-maker, John Harrison, invented a timepiece precise, balanced, and compact enough to work well on a ship. Chronometers, clocks designed for use at sea, continue to be highly collectible, and were often made in sets with barometers.

Telescopes were developed from the early 17th century by such renowned scientists as Galileo and Isaac Newton, but it was John Dolland in 1758 who discovered how to correct the distortion of the image caused by multiple lenses, and to create a large

rope handles on sea chests are called beckets and were sometimes made with elaborate braiding or macramé. This simple one, opposite, is joined to a carved wooden bracket on an English mahogany sea chest in the Granby collection.

enough field without having to use an overly long, unwieldy telescope. There are both terrestrial telescopes (for sighting boats and elements on land) and astronomical scopes (for stargazing). Spyglasses have several sections that collapse for portability (each section is called a draw), while telescopes have a single focusing tube and are often larger and mounted on tripods. Both types are generally made of brass, and antique models often have elegant barrel covers made of mahogany, leather, or sometimes shagreen.

The first marine barometer, which measures atmospheric pressure to help predict changes in the weather, was developed about 1773. Like land-based barometers, invented in the 17th century, it was comprised of a long, narrow column of mercury encased in glass, but it was mounted on gimbals and weighted at the base to keep it upright at sea. Round aneroid (liquid-free) barometers, more popular today, which look much like the chronometers (clocks) they're often paired with, measure pressure changes without the use of mercury.

maritime collecting at its finest, clockwise from top left: A matching Chelsea clock and barometer set from the 1920s. A brass ship's bell from the S.S. *Bremen,* a steamship ocean liner. A porthole window has come ashore, inset in a shed door. Brass bale pulls are flush with the front of an English mahogany campaign chest, circa 1860, for easier transport on a ship. A compass rose made of copper is inset into a modern-day deck. On this sailor-made sea chest, circa 1850, beautiful macramé rope beckets are fitted into an embossed leather bracket.

# navigating the past

Not all maritime collectors are sailors, and, of course, not all sailors are maritime collectors. Even fewer are boatbuilders and restorers as well as architectural restorers. Stephen Mack is all of these and more, and the knowledge he has gleaned in each of these roles enriches all of the others. He has sailed on tall ships, lived on a barge, and restored old wooden boats most of his adult life. He also rescues 18th-century houses, saving them from demolition by disassembling them, moving and storing them on his property, then rebuilding them on new sites, seamlessly integrating any new construction by using old materials and craftsmanship. At any given time, he may have as many as twenty-five different antique structures in storage on his fifty-acre property, Chase Hill Farm, in Rhode Island.

Restoring a fishing schooner years ago was his introduction to a lifelong passion for old wooden boats and the places where they still exist. His own house, which dates to 1792, is situated on a 50-acre farm near the sea in Rhode Island. It is a typical Cape Cod house with a center chimney and its original scrubbed oak floors, windows, and woodwork, which he stripped down to the original paint, adding a light coat of milk paint to preserve it. He moved all the other buildings to the farm from other locations, including a 50-foot barn that he uses as a boat workshop and a Rhode Island stone-ender house that serves as his office.

He chose the house because it hadn't been altered by renovations, only by age, and because it was in the perfect setting—near the water but surrounded by fields and bordered by a forest. Although he restores and designs houses for a living, he hasn't changed much about his own house. He believes that these houses are just like old wooden boats, with a certain charm and mystery and patina that comes with age.

Every object in Mack's house has a story—not just the story of its past, but often a complicated, candid, and entertaining story of how he acquired it. He will explain in detail how he found a huge,

nautical books, binoculars, a ship's log, and clocks, opposite, share space with a cast-iron tap from a huge 19th-century faucet, a Chinese export plate, and a French crystal clock on the set of hanging shelves Stephen Mack designed in 18th-century style for his library.

## seamen's chests

A sailor's chest was often his pride, his only piece of personal furnishing, where he stored his private belongings, or even sat in the evening. Early sea chests had wider bases, with sloping sides, to keep them from tipping over on high seas. They were sturdily built, often of pine, with dovetail joints and a skirt-board for extra protection around the base, and often painted on the outside. They were sometimes topped with canvas, which the sailor might take the time to decorate with knotwork or fringe, and fitted with decoratively knotted rope handles, or beckets, often looped through carved wooden brackets or cleats. Finer chests were made of teak or even mahogany, and not painted, except for the interior of the lid.

There are also many camphor chests (camphor has the same protective qualities as cedar) that were brought to the States through the China Trade in the 18th and 19th centuries. These were sometimes sold to sailors or used to crate precious cargo, and then sold again in port.

extremely heavy sailor's chest at a junk shop by a gas station and the melodrama that ensued as he tried to get it back to Rhode Island via Greyhound bus, or how he found a seaman's chest at the famous Brimfield flea market buried under metallic silver automobile paint. He didn't set out to amass the perfect maritime antiques collection; he has simply acquired items that have meaning to him, and carefully edited his possessions to work with the house and reflect his passions. It's not about amassing a complete collection of any particular genre, but about living with things that speak to the era of his house, the seafaring history of the region, and his own love of sailing, wooden boats, and the past.

Perhaps the most important part of his collection is his boats, including a 19th-century Cape Cod Sharpie, which is just what an oysterman of the period would have sailed in the shallow salt marshes in the area. The work Mack does restoring boats informs his work restoring and designing houses,

a captain's chair sits in front of the fire, opposite above. The woodwork throughout the house was stripped, then finished with a light, translucent coat of milk paint. The oak floorboards are original to the 1792 house. In a bedroom, opposite below, a 19th-century canvas chart case and some old charts sit atop a 19th-century sea chest with a charming heart-shaped whalebone escutcheon. Overleaf: A Windsor chair sits below a contemporary seascape by James Mitchell. The two 19th-century seamen's chests with their distinctive rope beckets (handles) seen in the adjoining room include a brass-bound camphor wood chest made in China and sold to sailors.

# sailing sayings

The English language is afloat with expressions that come from sailing. To name just a few:

- Stay afloat
- Stay on course
- The coast is clear
- Close quarters
- Batten down the hatches
- Go overboard
- On an even keel
- Knowing the ropes
- Safe passage
- When my ship comes in
- Clear the decks
- In the doldrums
- Give some leeway
- Give a wide berth
- Mainstay
- Miss the boat
- Ride out the storm
- Take the wind out of your sails
- Three sheets to the wind
- Are you on board?
- Uncharted waters
- Abandon ship
- Get your sea legs
- Steady as she goes
- High and dry
- Take a new tack
- Rudderless/adrift
- Heavy sailing
- Cast off
- Get/lose your bearings
- Lifesaver
- Windfall

and vice versa, making him especially fond of creating cozy spaces, tucking in extra storage, and using fine woods. He might build in a bank of mahogany drawers beside a bed, or add a set of small drawers inside a bookcase to create the sense of purpose melded with artistry that characterizes a fine yacht. Occasionally he uncovers elements in his house sleuthing that make the crossover more literally—for example, the 18th-century mast, now in his barn, that he found being used in an old house as a floor joist.

There is a sense of timelessness at Chase Hill Farm, so it's like stepping into a window on the past. Every object in the house and barns has been carefully chosen for its functionality and purity of design, and has a story of its own. Whether on water or land, he's found that the proportion that speaks to him is 18th and 19th century. The pace of life, the scent, the taste, the feel of that era is what feels just right.

## sailing sayings

- All hands on deck
- Tide over
- Bitter end
- Test the waters
- By and large
- Deep six
- With flying colors
- Different tack
- Fair-weather sailor
- Down the hatch
- First rate
- Get my drift?
- Don't give up the ship!
- Don't miss the boat
- Fly by night
- Under way
- Footloose
- Rummage
- Scuttlebutt
- Seaworthy
- Heads up
- Jump ship
- Hold the line
- First mate
- Ride out the storm
- Shipshape
- To fathom something
- Shipment
- Uncharted waters
- Water under the bridge
- Smooth sailing
- Tie up loose ends
- Take down a peg
- Under the weather

the simplicity and economy of a ship's galley are reflected in the kitchen, opposite, with open shelving for plates and cups and a rough-hewn granite sink unearthed in a frozen yard. The small casks, shipshape weathervane, and very old conch shells are subtle reminders of the sea. The countertops are antique chestnut floorboards and the faucet is 19th century. The copper ship's teakettle, below right, has a sturdy, broad base to keep it steady in swells. Even the gathered shower curtains, below left, have the feel of billowing sails. Whitewashed cedar boards repel water.

a stone-ender with a large Elizabethan pilaster
chimney stack, a type of house built in the late 17th and early
18th century in this area of Rhode Island, serves as an office.
Resting on the hearth of the large granite fireplace inside, opposite, is a bulwark cannon from a ship. An array of objects united
by their natural textures, including a woven fish creel and an iron
lantern, punctuates the rugged wooden beam.

# every ship has a story

Nearly every wall in Ken Martin and Nancy Burden's house in Maine is graced by portraits of sailing ships, their seaside backdrops reflecting the river view outside the windows, their rigging and flags each telling a story that is as compelling as the paintings themselves.

Martin's collection of more than 100 paintings and drawings of ships spans a wide range, from oil paintings of China Trade clipper ships to a watercolor sketchbook that is a visual diary of the ships one sailor encountered. For this former director of the Kendall Whaling Museum (now a part of the New Bedford Whaling Museum), much of the joy in acquiring a new picture is the tapestry of clues it offers to its subject—threads that he can then unravel through research to learn the name, nationality, size, and rigging of that particular ship, when it sailed, who were its captains and owners, what were its trade routes and cargo. Many ship's portraits were done for captains, officers, or owners, and identify their subject either through lettering on the ship itself, the signal flags it flies, or through information listed on the reverse of the painting, such as the name, captain or owner, date, home port, and so forth. A recognizable

harbor in the background offers clues as well. Even the portraits of ship captains, like many 19th-century portraits, often include a motif in the background, such as a small ship (or scales for a lawyer, for example), to indicate the subject's profession.

One of the wonderful things about the house is that it not only echoes the 19th-century period of the collections, but it was built by a sometime seafarer and carpenter who cobbled it together from parts of other houses and buildings he worked on. Many of the parts don't exactly match, and the house is out of plumb in places, but those are the kinds of idiosyncrasies that make a house like this unique and which have thankfully been preserved. The early-American furniture suits the house perfectly and adds to its historical resonance. And the way it is furnished isn't just for show: The 18th-century rope bed and Nova

watercolor portraits of commercial vessels in the living room, opposite, were found in a scrapbook that a painter made as a sort of "career biography" for a friend, illustrating the many ships he had skippered around the turn of the century. The pictures are conserved, matted, and framed with glass on both sides, so that the paintings on the reverse side can be seen as well.

Scotian fisherman's chest in the master bedroom are really used, the dining room is lit by candlelight, and the 19th-century globe in the library provides a world view circa 1867, useful in Martin's research.

The ship paintings, rather than crowding the walls, have been carefully grouped and hung to relate to one another thematically or artistically, and to suit the setting aesthetically. There are two paintings in an upstairs bedroom, for example, by two different sailors at two different times, and yet they share an amazing similarity of style and spirit. Clipper ship paintings are paired with tiny ship captain's portraits. A series of watercolor portraits in the living room are matted and framed in glass on both sides, because they came from a scrapbook and in some cases have pictures painted on the back as well. Fine examples of sailor's chests or ship models often sit beneath the paintings, forming harmonious vignettes. The collections of maritime antiques also include sand and log glasses, whaling logs, and scrimshaw whale's teeth, among other pieces.

clipper ships, left, that sailed to China in the 19th century were likely painted as portraits for visiting officers or captains in the ports of Hong Kong or Canton. To emphasize their shared spirit, they are in similar frames, balanced by two tiny portraits of ship's captains. The candle chandelier and sconce provide period-appropriate lighting in this dining room.

sand glasses, which measure some fraction of an hour, and smaller log glasses, used to measure the speed of a ship in 14- or 28-second intervals, above left, are gathered on pine shelves dating from 1820. A carved wooden sand glass whimsy, wooden school globe, a paraffin dipper made of whale ivory, and a sailor's ditty box mingle with antique books. A sailor's model of a five-masted schooner, below left, sits beneath a sailor-made painting of an imaginary five-masted bark (no such vessel ever existed). The New Hampshire rope bed, opposite, from the late 18th century is surrounded by ship portraits. The fisherman's chest and hooked rug are from the fishing port of Lunenburg in Nova Scotia, where sailing vessels were still being used until the middle of the 20th century. The five-pointed star resembles a compass rose, but is actually a common German decorative motif.

weathervanes

Weathervanes have been helping sailors determine the direction of the wind for millennia. In America, they became a form of folk art (and are now a valued collectible) with whimsical designs that often reflected commercial interests. In any seaside community, you are likely to find an enchanting range of simple sloops and cutter ships, whales, fish, and fishermen. Whether in flat relief cut from metal, like the fish below, or cast in a relief mold in copper, like the patinated sloop below left, or carved in wood, like the sailboat opposite, they are the perfect crowning touch to a waterfront home.

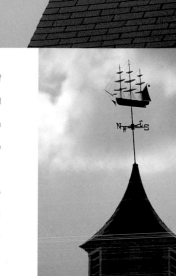

coastal
living

Lighthouses, boathouses, and sometimes even boats themselves: What they all offer that seems to appeal as much to our hearts as our minds is shelter. The cautioning, reassuring, lifesaving beacon that flashes across the sea, warning ships away from rocky coasts and unseen hazards, speaks to our

desire for security amid a sea of risk. The tall, stately cylindrical towers' form is synonymous with courage, perseverance, and protection. The solitary, steadfast lighthouse keeper, toiling day and night to keep the light burning and sound the foghorn, has assumed almost mythological status in our culture.

The boathouse, too, offers shelter from the storm, in an appealingly primitive, simplified version of a home—almost a kind of playhouse, sometimes adorned with whimsical gingerbread decoration, other times stripped down to the bare rafters and beams, as spare and functional as the planking and ribs of a wooden boat.

Boathouses, like lighthouses, are perched right on the cusp of the shore, inhabiting a tenuous middle ground between land and sea—and therein lies much of their appeal. Sleeping in or visiting one of the many boathouses, lighthouses, or keeper's cottages that have been reclaimed and renovated as homes offers both the serenity and the thrill of living directly on the water. Life is heightened here: Storms are more violent, sunrises and sunsets more dra-

matic, the stage set for nature more primal and more immediate.

The iconic image of the lighthouse is embedded in our individual and cultural imagination. Countless novels, paintings and photographs, travel guides, calendars, and even songs depict and celebrate the lighthouse; websites, stores, and numerous societies dedicated to the preservation of lighthouses, both in America and abroad, attest to its popularity. At one time, more than 1,200 lighthouses and beacons protected the United States coast alone. Today, nearly 600 are still standing, some operating as automated navigational aids; others are pre-

the unstudied ease of true sailing style, opposite: A bright yellow slicker is left to dry on a weathered once-white bench that is slowly turning the color of driftwood. Overleaf, left: The classic conical masonry lighthouse, with broad red and white stripes for visibility, stands sentry in various permutations up and down the Eastern seaboard. The New London Ledge Light, right, has the appearance of a grand Second Empire mansion adrift in the sea. Built in 1909, it is still in use today with an automated beacon. Local lore claims it is haunted by the ghost of a former keeper.

served as historic sites, parks, museums, or private homes, with nearly 250 open to the public (see "Resources" for more details). More than 100 lighthouses, lifesaving stations, ships, and shipwrecks have been designated and preserved as National Historic Landmarks, an acknowledgment of the important role these places have played in our history. Lighthouses are a visual emblem of our seafaring heritage, an embodiment of the adventure and courage inherent in our nation's culture.

As with nautical instruments, the architecture and design of lighthouses reflect advances in science and engineering that allowed for improved means of illumination, and for taller and sturdier lighthouses to be built on increasingly challenging sites, whether in water (wave-swept lighthouses) or on solid rock.

Boston Harbor Light, built in 1716, was the first American lighthouse. It suffered several fires (a hazard for all lighthouses before electrification), then was blown up by the British in 1776. A 75-foot octagonal tower replaced it in 1783 and is still in operation; because of its historical significance, this lighthouse is the only station in the country manned by resident Coast Guard keepers. The one pre-Revolutionary lighthouse that remains standing is at Sandy Hook, at the entrance to New York Harbor in New Jersey.

While the earliest lighthouses were often built of readily available wood, wood was not as durable as stone and was vulnerable to fire. Soon, stone and brick towers predominated because they could better withstand storms and severe weather. Later, cast iron, steel, and, eventually, reinforced concrete were used. The gently tapering conical design that is so distinctive to lighthouses evolved because it created even weight distribution for greater stability; its smooth contours minimized wind resistance and wave damage; and it allowed for tall towers—as much as 100 to 150 feet high. The optimal site for a lighthouse was high on a cliff (which accounts for the dramatic rocky coastal profile of many lighthouses), because the light needed to be high enough that it could be seen clearly from miles away at sea, despite the natural curvature of the earth.

Octagonal, square, and pyramidal structures became more common in the United States in the mid-19th century, as more harbor, rather than coastal, lights were built in more sheltered locations where simpler, more compact designs would suffice. In the Victorian era, there was a more eclectic range of styles, and inland lighthouses were often

boathouses, like lighthouses, are sometimes brightly colored to make them more visible from the water. The small red shed, opposite, above, built right on a dock, holds boating equipment and a small dinghy. Also perched right on the water, this stately white lighthouse and keeper's house, below, is picture-postcard New England with its tree-ringed setting. Overleaf: A cedar-shingle boathouse is reflected in the water, left, while a weathered white clapboard boathouse, right, sits by the water's edge.

simply a short tower attached or adjacent to the keeper's cottage. Many were modeled after traditional Nantucket, Cape Cod, and New England houses, though everything from Romanesque stone to Italianate brick to wooden Stick Style lighthouses can be found. Even the Statue of Liberty was originally used as a navigational aid.

Boathouses were (and still are) built as either sheds on the water with slips inside for day-to-day storage of boats, such as motor launches, or small houses on land meant for over-winter dry-dock storage. The latter might have ramps leading up from the water to the boathouse or davits or pulleys to lift the boats, or they might just rely on manpower to transfer the boat from water to shed. Boathouses on many lakes, harbors, and rivers have become miniature architectural masterpieces designed to echo either the larger houses they accompany or provide whimsical counterpoints, either of which makes viewing them from the water a pleasure and often a cruising destination.

The sometimes remote locations of lighthouses and boathouses can make them more challenging to live in, but that is part of their appeal. Despite any difficulties inherent in their upkeep and access, boathouses, lighthouse keeper's cottages, boat-building sheds, and other harbor buildings are gaining a second lease on life as residences, inns, and stores in coastal communities. People, it seems, will always be drawn to live by the shore.

# water's edge

In the kitchen of this converted boathouse on the shore of Martha's Vineyard, there are four notches on the door frame, each marking the height of the water that flooded the house during four different hurricanes—in 1938, 1944, and two in 1954. Finally, the next owner of the house raised it five feet and put it on pilings, and it hasn't been under water since. That doesn't mean the former boathouse hasn't weathered its share of storms, however. During the last big hurricane, the homeowners evacuated to a friend's house on higher ground, then returned to find a 37-foot sailboat moored on their roof, its rigging ripping up the roof boards, and another boat marooned on their dock. But their little house survived, just as it has for the past 75 years.

The shingle-clad cottage, with its big white batten doors and shutters, retains the simple, bare-bones appeal of a classic summer house, where furnishings are simple and functional. One table in the house was made from a board and an oar that came in through the window during one of the 1954 hurricanes, a kind of testament to the house's rugged seaworthiness.

The white-painted beaded-board cabinetry, sim-ple oyster-shell palette, summer white sheets and upholstery, set against the boathouse's original wooden floors and weathered shingles, evokes the simplicity of sailboats as well as the timeless, unpretentious style that makes summer living so appealing. A once-white bench has been left to weather naturally outdoors; a hemp rope serves as a handrail on narrow steps, just as it might on a boat.

The boathouse boasts prevailing salt-air breezes, breathtaking sunsets over the Edgartown harbor, the open invitation of a dock and mooring that encourage boating friends to drop a line and visit, and a relaxed informality that makes them want to stay.

While many boathouses, particularly on lakes, became obsolete when motorboats gained in popu-

a memento of storms past, the table was fashioned from a board that washed up into the house during a hurricane, opposite. It is flanked by easygoing canvas deck chairs. Surrounded by water, the porch feels like the deck of a boat, a feeling enhanced by the worn blue oar leaning against the storm shutters. Overleaf: Sailing friends and even long-lost acquaintances often ask to use the mooring or dock outside the boathouse. Its long, low roofline provides protection during the strong storms that often batter the coast.

## nantucket lightship baskets

In addition to lighthouses built on or near land, lightships were deployed starting in 1828 off the coast of Nantucket. At the South Shoal Lightship off Sankaty Head, the crews began weaving baskets to relieve the tedium of their four-month watches, developing the beautifully crafted, exceedingly sturdy oval or round basket known as a Nantucket lightship basket. From the 1860s on, they were shaped over an oval or round mold, with a base originally made of pine, but later of maple, cherry, or oak, with hickory or ash rims and handles. The sailors began making graduated sets of as many as eight baskets in distinctive fitted "nests," ranging in size from "a pint to a peck and a half," as one sailor put it. In about 1900, when the government discouraged basketweaving for fear that it interfered with the sailors' duties, the basketmaking moved ashore, and the original lightship crews trained the locals in their craft. Today, a new generation of craftspeople continues the tradition of these exquisite handwoven baskets.

larity during the 1930s, in the 1970s and 80s, people began renovating them, sometimes adding or converting a second story to create a guesthouse, and even building boathouses anew. The former stepchildren of grander houses became appreciated for their snug, small sense of scale and ease of care. As one owner put it, "What happened in our boathouse is that we planned the space perfectly for weekend guests, then spent one night in it ourselves, listening to the water, and we never moved back to the cottage."

As the sometimes remote locations of these rehabbed buildings, such as Coast Guard lifesaving stations, coaling stations, and lighthouses, can make them more challenging to bring supplies to, and because these structures are usually close to the shore, the size and type of renovation that can be done is also often restricted. And if the unusual shapes and diminutive sizes of some boathouses and lighthouses further add to the challenges, they also account for their uncommon beauty.

a cape dory 10, opposite, a simple 10-foot skiff that can be rowed, sailed, or powered by motor, has been in the family for nearly 30 years. Overleaf: The cast-iron sink, original to the house, left, is deep enough to hold flower buckets. The beaded-board cabinetry was added more recently, but it perfectly suits the style of the 1920s house. Right: A white beach rose, a hurricane-shaded candle nestled in a bed of sand, and an old-fashioned blackboard are the essence of sailing style.

# the perfect mooring

Sailing is a passport to some of the most pictur-esque, unspoiled, out-of-the-way places that have been attracting sailors for generations. The coast of Maine is dotted with many such inviting harbors and tiny islands. Like other longtime sailing communities (such as Marblehead, Massachusetts; Newport, Rhode Island; Martha's Vineyard, and Nantucket), coastal Maine's jewels, such as Camden, Rockport, Northeast Harbor, Kennebunkport, Southwest Har-bor, Bar Harbor, North Haven, and here, along Penobscot Bay, offer choice destinations for both competitive and recreational sailors.

It all started with the abundance of towering ever-green forests in this state that spawned a thriving boatbuilding industry (trees provided not only lumber for ships, but also shingles, barrel staves, and pine

pitch) that lives on today. Even when ships began being made of iron rather than wood, the Bath Iron Works kept Maine in the forefront of boat construc-tion. As sailors rediscover the beauty of wooden and custom-built boats, the preponderance of premier craftsmen and boatyards, such as the distinguished Hinckley Company in Southwest Harbor, and wooden boatbuilding schools, such as the WoodenBoat School in Brooklin, can still be found in Maine.

The sailing ports of rocky Maine are completely different in character from the more shallow, sandy beach coasts of much of Long Island and Cape Cod, which in turn differ dramatically from harbors in more tropical locales such as the British Virgin Islands—and it is that variety that makes sailing such a com-pelling means of travel, one that always offers the thrill of new discoveries.

One small island off the coast north of Camden even boasts its own special class of sailboats, Dark Harbor 20s, which are raced only here on this island. The tradition began in the early 1900s, and in 1935, the legendary Olin Stephens, then just a fledging yacht designer, was commissioned to design the Dark Harbor 20. Twenty-one of these boats were

a boathouse has been renovated for year-round living, opposite. The cedar shingles and dark green awnings reflect the palette of the rocky Maine coast and the sheltering pines that surround the house on the water's edge. Overleaf: The owner's 1937 wooden Dark Harbor 20 sloop was as lovingly restored as the boathouse. The second-story tower, flanked by outdoor decks, is the bedroom addition. The awnings add to its traditional Down East summer cottage appeal.

# wisdom of the sea

Your house shall not be an anchor but a mast.

—**Khalil Gibran**


Blue sky at night, sailors delight.
Red sky in morning, sailors take warning.

—**Anonymous**


The sea is all about us.

—**T. S. Eliot**


Was there ever a sailor free to choose that
didn't settle somewhere near the sea?

—**Rudyard Kipling**


Like unto ships far off at sea outward or
homeward bound are we.

—**Henry Wadsworth Longfellow**


If a man must be obsessed by something,
I suppose a boat is as good as anything,
perhaps a bit better than most.

—**E. B. White**


or whatever we lose (like a you or a me)
it's always ourselves we find in the sea.

—**e. e. cummings**


The ocean and its treasures are the common
property of all men.

—**John Adams**


There is a witchery in the sea, its songs and
stories.

—**Richard Henry Dana**

built, and more than sixty-five years later, twenty of them are still raced every Wednesday and Saturday throughout the summer.

This century-old boathouse on 12 acres of land along the water's edge was restored and rebuilt simultaneously with the restoration of a wooden Dark Harbor 20 sloop. Both were labors of love, and each without question complements the other.

The boathouse was small and sparsely equipped, but the footprint had to be maintained in order to preserve its precious location just 12 feet from the shore. (Zoning requires any new building to be set back at least 75 feet from the water.) Renovated, winterized, and slightly expanded by adding a second-floor bedroom and deck, the resulting house is still just 650 square feet. Sailboats were the inspiration to make the most of every inch. In the bedroom, not much bigger than a boat cabin, a captain's bed was built in with drawers underneath for storage. The compact kitchen is styled like an old ship's galley,

the deck on the second story, opposite above, for dining or relaxing, gives the sense of being on the deck of a boat, surrounded by calming views of the water and the blue silhouette of the Camden Hills in the distance. The salt air tinged with the pungent scent of balsam and pine is that refreshing fragrance known as coastal Maine. The kitchen table, opposite below, offers the same captivating view out its bank of three windows. Overleaf: In the living room, honeyed pine beaded-board paneling trimmed in dark green and a fieldstone fireplace give this boathouse a rugged demeanor, balanced by the softer, lighter touches of awning-striped and checked upholstery.

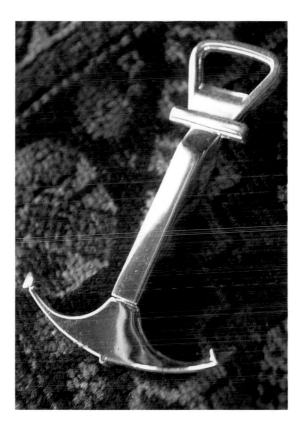

nautical charts and a 19th-century barometer and clock, with binoculars perched by the window, opposite, hint at the sea in this camplike cottage. A well-loved antique leather wing chair with a rug-covered cushion is the best place to keep an eye on the weather. The silver anchor bottle opener, above, is another reference to sailing.

with copper counters, and the living room is lined with pine beaded-board paneling in the style of an antique boat interior. Set among towering pines, with its tall fieldstone fireplace and dark green trim, it combines boathouse living with Maine lodge style.

The interior is casual in summer, and cozy, warm, and weather-tight in winter, which in Maine is three seasons of the year. The yellow-and-white-striped upholstery is warmed up by antique Oriental rugs and a worn leather wing chair. The rugged fireplace offers a welcome respite for the chilled and weary sailor at night, and is a source of warmth and light on long winter nights. Roman shades let in the view during the day, but drawn at night, add a sense of security and warmth. In summer, the second-story decks flanking the bedroom, the dining porch (screened in summer, glassed-in in winter, but unheated and unelectrified, so dining is by romantic candlelight), and abundance of windows framing the coastal views keep the house light and open to the water.

Evergreen awnings complement the cedar shingles and hunter trim, adding to the old-fashioned summerhouse effect. Nautical charts of the island and Maine coast, whaling prints, a 19th-century barometer and clock, the ever-present binoculars, and even small touches like a silver anchor bottle opener are all subtle reminders of the sailing life. And with the harbor as a front yard, and a sailboat moored right outside the door, the sea is never more than a step away.

# to the lighthouse

A mile away from Newport, Rhode Island, in Narragansett Bay, the Rose Island Lighthouse, built in 1869, stands almost completely apart from time. When you take the short ferry ride over to the island, which is populated predominantly by herons, egrets, and other species of birds, you step back to 1912, the period to which the lighthouse has been restored, with very little to break the mesmerizing spell of this enchanted location. Saved from developers by a preservation- and environmentally minded group of local citizens in 1984, who labored for years to completely clean and renovate the heavily damaged and vandalized structure, the decommissioned lighthouse was relit (as a private aid to navigation) in 1993. The 16-acre island (now completely owned by the Rose Island Lighthouse Foundation) was used in the 1770s through the early 1800s as a British, French, and then American fort (the stone bastions can still be seen encircling the lighthouse), and later, in World Wars I and II, as a naval torpedo station and ammunitions dump.

This extraordinary place is the only lighthouse where you can not only sleep overnight, but serve as the keeper as well. Paying guests sign up for week-long stints as the lighthouse keeper, helping to maintain the house and grounds, keep the log, and work on building and landscaping projects. Or you can stay in the first-floor "living museum" as an overnight guest. The self-sufficient lighthouse is also designed to serve as a hands-on lesson in eco-aware living (much as it was for the lighthouse keepers of the past century): The water supply comes from rainwater collected in a cistern; electricity is provided by windmill and solar batteries, and the 20-amp service allows for a refrigerator and lights, but not much else. The saying at Rose Island is: "If it's windy, vacuum. If it's not, sweep." Everything must be packed in and

adirondack chairs at Rose Island, opposite, built by a local Boy Scout troop from donated mahogany, are typical of the ingenuity and generosity that has kept the lighthouse foundation alive and thriving. The board-and-batten door (used to "batten down the hatches" in a storm), the clapboard siding of the keeper's house, and an iron railing on the rocky fortress's perimeter demonstrate the similar ways in which both coastal buildings and boats were designed to weather strong winds and high seas. Overleaf: The 1869 French Empire Revival house, with its square light tower, and oil house and doghouse beside it, stand guard on the outcropping of circular stone bastions built as a British fort in the 1770s.

# resources:
# when your ship comes in

## ship's chandlery

### marine supplies

**Barkley Sound Oar & Paddle Ltd.**
3073 Van Horne Road
Qualicum Beach, BC
Canada V9K 1X3
250-752-5115
www.barkleysoundoar.com
Oars and paddles

**Best Marine Imports, Inc.**
1749 East Hallandale Beach Blvd.
Hallandale, FL 33009
954-805-0782
888-784-8611
www.bestmarineimports.com
Anchors, pumps, repair kits,
accessories

**Classic Marine**
Lime Kiln Quay
Woodbridge, Suffolk IP12 1BD
England
011 44 1394 380390
www.classicmarine.co.uk
Blocks, custom sailing equipment,
rigging

**Downwind Maine—The Cruiser's
Chandler**
2804 Canon Street
San Diego, CA 92106
619-224-2733
www.downwindmarine.com
Marine supplies

**Mast Mate**
21 Ocean Street
Rockland, ME 04841
800-548-0436
www.mastmate.com
Blocks and tackle

**Mott's Marine Supplies**
Route 1
Newcastle, ME 04553
207-563-5555
www.mottsmarinesalvage.com
Buoys and traps

**New England Traditional Boat, LLC**
P.O. Box 214
Southwest Harbor, ME 04679
(207) 244-0003
www.traditionalboat.com
Blockmaker and chandlery

**New York Nautical**
140 West Broadway
New York, NY 10013
212-962-4522
www.newyorknautical.com
Instruments and charts

**Paul E. Luke, Inc.**
15 Luke's Gulch
East Boothbay, ME 04544
207-633-4971
207-633-3388
www.peluke.com
Marine hardware and services

**S. T. Preston & Sons, Inc.**
Main Street Wharf
Greenport, NY 11944
631-477-1990
www.prestons.com
Marine supplies, charts, fishing tackle,
marine books, ship models

**Van Cort Instruments**
110 Lyman Street
Holyoke, MA 01040
413-538-9100
800-432-2678
www.vancort.com
Reproduction instruments

**West Marine**
P.O. Box 50070
Watsonville, CA 95077
800-262-8464
www.westmarine.com
Marine supplies

## paint and varnishes

**Daly's Paint**
3525 Stone Way North
Seattle, WA 98103
206-633-4200
www.dalyspaint.com
Teak oil finish

**Epifanes North America, Inc.**
70 Water Street
Thomaston, ME 04861
207-354-8004
800-269-0961
www.epifanes.com
Paint and varnish

**Interlux**
International Paint Inc.
2270 Morris Avenue
Union, NJ 07083
908-686-1300
908-686-8545
www.yachtpaint.com

**George Kirby, Jr. Paint Co.**
163 Mount Vernon Street
New Bedford, MA 02740
508-997-9008
www.kirbypaint.com

**Penofin Performance Coating**
800-PENOFIN
800-736-6346
www.penofin.com
(store locator available online)
Wood stain

**Woolsey Paint**
Available at: Kop Coat, Inc.
412-227-2700
www.kop-coat.com

## ropes

**Allen C. Rawl, Inc.—Spinflex Rope**
11314 Reynolds Road
Bradshaw, MD 21087
410-592-2170
www.shipsofwood.com

There are only two colors to paint a boat, black or white, and only a fool would paint a boat black.

—Nathanael G. Herreshoff

**New England Rope**
Available at: Sailnet
3864 Leeds Avenue
N. Charleston, SC 29405
800-234-3220
www.sailnet.com

## nautical hardware
**J. M. Reineck & Son**
9 Willow Street
Hull, MA 02045
781-925-3312
www.bronzeblocks.com
Nautical hardware

## sailmakers and upholsterers
**All the King's Flags**
2000 NW Market Street
Seattle, WA 98107
2707 Congress Street
San Diego, CA 92110
800-255-3690

**Bacon and Associates**
116 Legion Avenue
Annapolis, MD 21401
410-263-4880
www.baconsails.com

**Halsey Lidgard (Sailmakers)**
Seattle, WA
206-632-2609
www.halseylidgardpacific.com

**Lee Sails**
WA: 800-533-9567
OR: 503-641-7170
www.leesails.com

**North Sails**
80 Mid Tech Drive, #10
West Yarmouth, MA 02673
508-778-6550
www.northsails.com

**Sail Swap**
1206A FM 2094
Kemah, TX 77565
281-455-0535
www.sailswaptexas.com
Buy and sell used sails

**Shilshole Upholstery and Leather Works**
6711 21 Avenue NW
Seattle, WA 98117
206-781-9322

**UK Sailmakers**
108 Severn Avenue
Annapolis, MD 21403
410-268-1175
800-253-2002
www.uksailmakers.com

## maritime arts
**Alison Langley Photography**
81 West Commercial Street
Portland, ME 04101
207-774-2551
www.langleyphoto.com
Sailing photography

**American Marine Model Gallery**
12-M Derby Square
Salem, MA 01970
978-745-5777
www.shipmodel.com
Ship models

**Atlas Gallery**
49 Dorset Street
London W14 7NF
England
011 44 207 324 4192
www.atlasgallery.com
Sailing photography

**Godel & Co.**
39A East 72nd Street
New York, NY 10021
212-288-7272
19th- and 20th-c. American oil paintings

**The Lannan Ship Model Gallery**
540 Atlantic Avenue
Boston, MA 02110
617-451-2650
www.lannangallery.com
Models, paintings, signs

**Michael Kahn Photography**
**Gardner Colby Gallery**
27 North Water Street
Edgartown, MA 02539
508-627-6002
www.gardnercolbygallery.com
Contemporary sepia sailing photographs

**North Star Galleries**
3 East 76th Street
New York, NY 10021
212-794-4277
and
105 Spring Street
Newport, RI 02840
401-846-7200
www.northstargallery.com
Ship models

## antiques
**English Country Antiques**
Snake Hollow Road
Bridgehampton, NY 11932
631-537-0606
Sailboat and pond models

**Hyland Granby Antiques**
P.O. Box 457
Hyannis Port, MA 02647
508-771-3070
Fine maritime antiques

**John F. Rinaldi**
P.O. Box 765
Kennebunkport, ME 04046
207-967-3218
Antique scrimshaw, ship models,
paintings. By appointment.

**John T. Newton**
P.O. Box 247
New Castle, ME 04538
207-563-8591
Fine maritime antiques by appointment

**Louis J. Dianni**
P.O. Box 458
Sherman, CT 06784
800-694-1421
Maritime antiques, ship
models, artifacts

**Mare Nostrum**
6600 Route 219
P.O. Box 1746
Ellicottville, NY 14731
716-699-5279
Custom orders as well as hull models,
model ships, and maps

## paint

**Benjamin Moore Exterior Ready-Mix**
Sail Cloth

**Benjamin Moore Interior Paints**

| | |
|---|---|
| Sea Wind | OC-139 |
| Seashell | OC-120 |
| Powder Sand | OC-113 |
| Whitewater Bay | OC-70 |
| Seapearl | OC-19 |
| Maritime White | OC-5 |
| Blue Wave | 2065-50 |
| Clearest Ocean Blue | 2064 40 |
| Sailor's Sea Blue | 2063-40 |
| Old Navy | 2063-10 |
| Harbor Fog | 2062-70 |
| Tidal Wave | 2061-50 |
| Seaport Blue | 2060-30 |
| Marine Blue | 2059-10 |
| Ocean Breeze | 2058-60 |
| Deep Ocean | 2058-30 |
| Bahamian Sea Blue | 2055-40 |
| Caribbean Blue Water | 2055-30 |
| Pacific Ocean Blue | 2055-20 |
| Seaside Blue | 2054-50 |
| Blue Seafoam | 2056 60 |
| Beacon Gray | 2128-60 |
| Anchor Gray | 2126-30 |
| Seafoam | 2123-60 |
| Ocean Air | 2123-50 |
| Whitewater | 2120-60 |
| Sea Life | 2118-40 |
| Stone Harbor | 2111-50 |

**Benjamin Moore Outdoor Deck
Satin Paints**
Maritime White

**Martha Stewart Everyday Colors
Interior Paints**
Drop Of Blue
Bluepoint

**Martha Stewart and Fine Paints of
Europe Skylands Colors**

| | |
|---|---|
| Sea Lavender | 27 |
| High Tide | 7 |
| Flying Jib | 6 |

**Martha Stewart Schreuder
Interior Paints**

| | |
|---|---|
| North Sea Blue | 7025 |
| Fisherman's Blue | 4040-D |

**Martin Senour Interior Paints**

| | |
|---|---|
| Seaside | 154-6 (WW) |
| All Ashore | 111-6 (WW) |
| Coast to Coast | 226-3 |
| Freshwater | 225-3 |
| Frothy Seas | 221-1 |
| Windward Sails | 221-2 |

**Pittsburgh Interior Paints**

| | |
|---|---|
| Washed Sand | 2520 |
| Bar Harbor | 2043 |
| Shipmate Blue | 2082 |
| Windswept | 2555 |
| Sea Fleur | 2564 |

**Schreuder and Fine Paints of Europe
Interior Paints**

| | |
|---|---|
| Blue Horizon | 4022 |
| North Sea Blue | 7025 |

**Sherwin Williams Interior Paints**

| | |
|---|---|
| Tide Pool | SW1754 |
| Wild Surf Blue | SW1755 |
| Nautical Blue | SW1763 |
| Bluepoint | SW1758 |
| Ocean View | SW1705 |
| Newport Blue | SW2264 |
| Bar Harbor | SW2272 |

**Ralph Lauren Whitewash Collection**

| | |
|---|---|
| Storm Lightning | WW47 |
| Sail White | WW49 |
| Breakwater White | WW62 |
| Cove Point | WW29 |
| White Heron | WW30 |
| Sailor's Knot | WW15 |
| Montauk Driftwood | WW19 |

**Ralph Lauren Sea & Sky**

| | |
|---|---|
| Seven Seas | SS38 |
| Spinnaker | SS31 |
| Coast | SS72 |
| Ocean Spray | SS68 |
| Dock Blue | SS23 |
| Schoal Water | SS04 |
| Fog | SS08 |
| Tidewater | SS63 |
| Northeast Harbour | SS47 |
| Northern Lights | SS48 |
| North Haven | SS41 |
| Sea Mist | SS46 |
| Seasport | SS51 |
| Wickford Bay | SS54 |

## fabrics

**Perennials—"Sailor's Collection"**
888-322-4773
www.perennialsfabric.com
Striped and solid outdoor fabrics

**Sunbrella**
Glen Raven Custom Fabrics, LLC
1831 North Park Avenue
Glen Raven, NC 27217
336-221-2211
www.sunbrella.com
Outdoor fabrics in stripes and solids

**Umbra**
1705 Broadway
Buffalo, NY 14212
800-387-5122
www.umbra.com
Natural canvas shades with grommets

## furnishings

**Authentic Models**
"Starbay Collection"
P.O. Box 21710
Eugene, OR 97402
800-888-1992
888-GARFIELD
www.authenticmodels.com
Rosewood sea captain's furniture

**Ibolili**
104 Leonard Drive
Greensboro, NC 27410
866-426-5454
ibolili@aol.com
Rope furnishings

**L. L. Bean**
800-441-5713
www.llbean.com
Rope hammock, canvas bags

**Nantucket Knotworks**
3 Sparrow Drive
Nantucket, MA 02554
508-228-7107
www.nantucketknotworks.com
Rope accessories for home and yacht

**Nautica Home**
www.nautica.com
Sheets, towels, furniture

**Ralph Lauren Home Collection**
212-642-8700
www.poloralphlauren.com
Sheets, towels, fabric, wallcoverings

### nautical house hardware

**Brass 'N Bounty**
68 Front Street
Marblehead, MA 01945
781-631-3864
www.brassandbounty.com
Brass hardware and fittings

**Eighteenth Century Hardware**
131 East Third Street
Derry, PA 15627
724-694-2708
Anchor door knocker

**Harbor Farm**
P.O. Box 64
Little Deer Isle, ME 04650
207-348-7737
www.harborfarm.com
Ships hooks and hardware

### fashion

**Brooks Brothers**
800-274-1815
www.brooksbrothers.com
Navy blazer

**Garnet Hill**
800-870-3513
www.garnethill.com
French sailor shirts

**J. Peterman**
888-647-2555
www.jpeterman.com
Russian navy shirts

**Keds**
800-680-0966
www.keds.com
Canvas boat sneakers

**Lands' End**
800-356-4444
www.landsend.com
Slickers, canvas bags, deck shoes

**Rockport**
800-762-5767
www.rockport.com
Deck shoes

**Sperry Top-Sider**
800-617-2239
www.sperrytopsider.com
Deck shoes

**Team One Newport**
P.O. Box 1443
Newport, RI 02840
800-847-4327
www.team1newport.com
Brenton Red pants

**Vermont Bird Co.**
71 Olive Court
Mountain View, CA 94041
415-967-3123
Cashmere watch caps

## ports of call

### maritime museums
CONNECTICUT
**Mystic Seaport Museum**
75 Greenmanville Avenue
Mystic, CT 06355
860-572-0711
888-973-2767
www.mysticseaport.org

MAINE
**The Farnsworth Art Museum**
Wyeth Collection
352 Main Street
Rockland, ME 04841
207-596-6457
www.farnsworthmuseum.org

**Maine Maritime Museum**
243 Washington Street
Bath, ME 04530
207-443-1316
www.bathmaine.com

**Penobscot Marine Museum**
Church Street, Route 1
P.O. Box 498
Searsport, ME 04974
207-548-2529
www.penobscotmarine
museum.org

"To sail is the thing," wrote Arthur Ransome in his children's classic, *Swallows and Amazons*. And just what is that thing? Every sailor knows. It's what the poets say and the pictures show, and everything else, too; it's the joy of casting off and the delight of returning home, and it's all the winds and the waves in between. It's the beauty of a boat and the power of the currents, the sound of ratcheting winches and the strain on the wheel; it's the fair breezes and sunsets, the storms and luffing sails. It's the beer in the bar when the race is done, and that moment when you feel you'll never get there. It's what sailors mean when, safe and dry, standing on solid ground, they look at you and say, "I'd rather be sailing."

—Anne Depue

MARYLAND
**Chesapeake May Maritime Museum**
Mill Street
St. Michaels, MD 21663
410-745-2098
www.cbmm.org

MASSACHUSSETS
**Captain Forbes House Museum**
215 Adams Street
Milton, MA 02186
617-696-1815
www.key-biz.com/ssn/milton/forbes

**Essex Shipbuilding Museum**
668-28 Main Street
Essex, MA 01929
978-768-7541
www.essexshipbuildingmuseum.org

**Hart Nautical Gallery at
M.I.T. Museum**
55 Massachusetts Avenue
Cambridge, MA 02138
617-253-4444
www.mit.edu

**The Museum of Boston Harbor
Heritage**
Hull Lifesaving Museum
1117 Nantasket Avenue
Hull, MA 02045
781-925-5433

**Nantucket Lightship Basket Museum**
P.O. Box 2517
Nantucket, MA 02584
508-228-1177

**New Bedford Whaling Museum**
18 Johnny Cake Hill
New Bedford, MA 02740
508-997-0046
www.whalingmuseum.org

**Peabody Essex Museum**
East India Square
Salem, MA 01970
978-745-9500
800-745-4054
www.pem.org

**Salem Maritime National
Historic Site**
174 Derby Street
Salem, MA 01970
978-740-1650
www.nps.gov/sama

**Sleeper–McCann Historic House**
75 Eastern Point Blvd.
Gloucester, MA 01930
978-283-0800

NEW YORK
**Cold Spring Harbor Whaling
Museum**
Main Street
P.O. Box 25
Cold Spring Harbor, NY 11724
631-367-3418
www.cshwhalingmuseum.org

**Hudson River Maritime Museum**
1 Rondout Landing
Kingston, NY 12401
845-338-0071
www.ulster.net/~hrmm

**Long Island Maritime Museum**
P.O. Box 184
86 West Avenue
West Sayville, NY 11796
631-HISTORY
www.limaritime.org

**The Sag Harbor Whaling Museum**
200 Main Street
Sag Harbor, NY 11963
631-725-0770
www.sagharborwhalingmuseum.org

PENNSYLVANIA
**Independence Seaport Museum**
211 S. Columbus Blvd. and Walnut
   Street
Philadelphia, PA 19106
215-925-5439
www.phillyseaport.org

RHODE ISLAND
**Herreshoff Marine Museum**
1 Burnside Street
Bristol, RI 02809
401-253-5000
www.ohwy.com/ri/h/
   herrmamu.htm

**The Museum of Newport History**
127 Thames Street
Newport, RI 02840
401-841-8770

**The Museum of Yachting**
Ft. Adams State Park
P.O. Box 129
Newport, RI 02840
401-847-1018
www.moy.org

**Naval War College Museum**
686 Cushing Road
Newport, RI 02841
401-841-4052
www.nwc.navy.mil/museum

**The Newport Historical Society**
82 Touro Street
Newport, RI 02840
401-846-0813
www.newporthistorical.com

VIRGINIA
**The Mariners' Museum**
100 Museum Drive
Newport News, VA 23606
800-581-7245
www.mariner.org

Twenty years from now, you will be more disappointed by the things you didn't do than by the ones you did do. So throw off the bowlines. Sail away from the safe harbor. Catch the trade winds in your sails. Explore. Dream. Discover.

—Mark Twain

WASHINGTON
**Gig Harbor Peninsula Museum**
4218 Harborview Drive
P.O. Box 744
Gig Harbor, WA 98335
253-858-6722
www.gigharbormuseum.org

**Westport Maritime Museum**
2201 Westhaven Drive
P.O. Box 1074
Westport, WA 98595-1074
360-268-0078
www.westportwa.com/museum

INTERNATIONAL
**Australian National Maritime Museum**
2 Murray Street
Darling Harbour NSW 2009
GPO Box 5131
Sydney NSW 1042
Australia
011 61 2 9298 3777
www.anmm.gov.au

**Danish Mercantile Maritime Museum**
Kronborg Slot
3000 Helsingor
Denmark
011 45 4928 0200
www.kulturnet.dk/homes/hsmk

**National Maritime Museum**
Romney Road
Greenwich, London
SE10 9NF
England
011 44 20 8858 4422
Information line:
011 44 20 8312 6565
www.nmm.ac.uk

**Netherlands Maritime Museum**
Kattenburgerplein 1
1018 KK Amsterdam
Netherlands
011 31 20 5232222
www.scheepvaartmuseum.nl

**Paris Marine Museum**
Palais de Chaillot
17 Place du Trocadéro
75116 Paris, France
011 53 65 6969
www.musee-marine.fr

## north atlantic lighthouses

CONNECTICUT
**Lighthouse Museum**
Water Street
Stonington, CT 06378
860-535-1440

**New Haven Harbor Point Lighthouse**
Lighthouse Park
New Haven, CT 06512

MAINE
**American Lighthouse Foundation**
P.O. Box 889
Wells, ME 04090
207-646-0515

**Cape Neddick Lighthouse**
Route 1
York, ME 03909
Chamber of Commerce
207-363-4422

**Lighthouse Depot**
U.S. Route 1 North
Wells, ME 04090
800-758-1444
www.lighthousedepot.com

MASSACHUSETTS
**Clark's Point Lighthouse**
Fort Taber Park
New Bedford, MA 02740

**Edgartown Lighthouse**
Martha's Vineyard Historical Society
Edgartown, MA 02539
508-627-4441

**Gay Head Lighthouse**
Martha's Vineyard Historical Society
Aquinnah Cliffs
Martha's Vineyard, MA 02543
508-627-4441

**Nobska Light**
Martha's Vineyard Historical Society
Woods Hole, MA 02543
508-627-4441

NEW YORK
**Fire Island Lighthouse**
4640 Captree Island
Captree Island, NY 11702
631-661-4876

**Horton Point Lighthouse**
Southold Historical Society
Lighthouse Road
Southold, NY 11971
631-765-5500

**Montauk Lighthouse**
Montauk Historical Society
Turtle Hill, Route 27
Montauk, NY 11954
631-668-2544

**National Lighthouse Museum**
1 Lighthouse Plaza
St. George, Staten Island, NY 10301
718-556-1681

RHODE ISLAND
**Rose Island Lighthouse**
P.O. Box 1419
Newport, RI 02840
401-847-4242

## sailing schools and classes
**American Sail Training Association**
P.O. Box 1459
Newport, RI 02852
401-846-1775
www.tallships.sailtraining.org

**The Carmens River Maritime Center and Boat Shop**
P.O. Box 204
Brookhaven Hamlet, NY 11719
631-286-0686
www.postmorrow.org

## charters and cruises

**Arabella**
800-395-1343
Newly refurbished, 160 feet, 22 staterooms; Martha's Vineyard, Cape Cod, Nantucket, Plymouth; in winter, the Caribbean

**American Eagle and Heritage Schooners**
P.O. Box 482
Rockland, ME 04841
207-594-8007
Three- to ten-day schooner trips

**Endeavor**
Slip #1015
Straight Wharf
P.O. Box 64
Nantucket Island, MA 02554
508-228-5585
www.endeavorsailing.com
Built by its captain, the longest-operating sailing charter on Nantucket

**The Liberty Fleet of Tall Ships**
67 Long Wharf
Boston, MA 02110
617-742-0333
www.libertyfleet.com
Daily sails and charters

**Northwest Schooner Society**
P.O. Box 9504
Seattle, WA 98109
206-633-2780
800-551-NWSS
www.nwschooner.org (donations)
Sponsors voyages through Washington State and British Columbia

**Sea Cloud Cruises**
201-227-9404
888-732-2568
www.seacloud.com
Ninety-six-passenger bark, forty-eight cabins, wood-paneled walls, marble bathtubs; cruise the Caribbean, the Baltic, the Mediterranean

**Schooner America**
31 Bowers Wharf
Newport, RI 02840
www.schooneramerica.com
Daily cruises and private charters

**The Egan Institute of Maritime Studies**
The Coffin School
4 Winter Street
Nantucket, MA 02554
508-228-2505
www.eganinstitute.com

**Offshore Sailing School**
Chelsea Piers
New York, NY 10011
212-627-SAIL
800-221-4326
www.chelseapiers.com/masailing.htm
www.offshore-sailing.com

**International Yacht Restoration School**
449 Thames Street
P.O. Box WB
Newport, RI 02840
401-848-5777
www.iyrs.com

**OP Sail, Inc.**
1299 Pennsylvania Ave, NW
9th Floor, Suite 960
Washington, DC 20004
202-638-1121
www.opsail.org

**Sea Education Association**
P.O. Box 6
Woods Hole, MA 02543
800-552-3633
www.sea.edu

**SUNY Maritime College**
6 Pennyfield Avenue
Throgs Neck, NY 10465
718-409-7200
800-654-1874
www.sunymaritime.edu

**U.S. Merchant Marine Academy**
300 Steamboat Road
Kings Point, NY 11024
516-773-5000
www.usmma.edu

**U.S. Naval Academy**
121 Blake Road
Annapolis, MD 21402
888-249-7709
www.usna.edu

**U.S. Coast Guard Auxiliary**
877-875-6296
www.cgaux.org

**WoodenBoat Foundation**
380 Jefferson Street
Port Townsend, WA 98368
360-385-3628
www.woodenboat.org

**WoodenBoat School**
Naskeag Road
P.O. Box 78
Brooklin, ME 04616
207-359-4651
www.woodenboat.com
Boatbuilding and sailing courses

## races and regattas

**America's Cup**
www.americascup.com

**Antigua Classic Yacht Regatta**
Antigua Yacht Club
268-460-1799
www.antiguaclassics.com

**Louis Vuitton Cup**
www.louisvuittoncup.com

**Opera House Cup Regatta**
The Coffin School
4 Winter Street
P.O. Box 2424
Nantucket, MA 02584
508-325-7755
www.operahousecup.com

## clubs

**Newport Yacht Club**
P.O. Box 488
Newport, RI 02840
401-846-9410
www.newportyachtclub.org

**New York Yacht Club**
37 West 44th Street
New York, NY 10036
212-382-1000
www.nyyc.org

**The Royal Corinthian Yacht Club**
The Parade
Cowes, Isle of Wight PO31 7QU
England
011 44 1983 293581
www.royalcorinthian.co.uk

**The Royal Yacht Squadron**
The Castle
Cowes, Isle of Wight PO31 7QT
England
011 44 1983 292191
www.rys.org.uk
www.cowes.co.uk

**St. Francis Yacht Club**
On the Marina
San Francisco, CA 94123
415-563-6363
www.stfyc.com

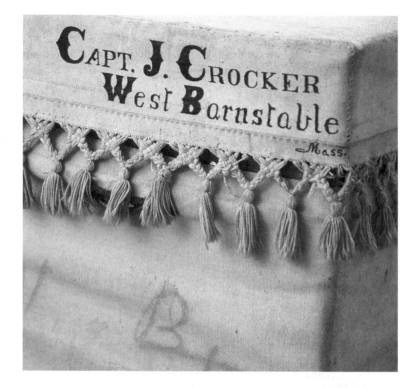

## yacht designers

**Brooklin Boatyard**
Center Harbor Road
Brooklin, ME 04616
207-359-2236
E. B. White family business

**Cape Cod Shipbuilding**
P.O. Box 152
7 Narrows Road
Wareham, MA 02571
508-295-3550
www.four.net/~ccsb/ccsbhp.html
Builders of Herreshoff yachts

**The Eric Dow Boatshop**
P.O. Box 7
Brooklin, ME 04616
207-359-2277
Joel White designs

**Farr Yacht Design, Ltd.**
P.O. Box 4964
613 Third Street, Suite 20
Annapolis, MD 21403
410-267-0780
www.farrdesign.com
Designers of high performance and
racing yachts

**Hinckley Company**
P.O. Box 699
130 Shore Road
Southwest Harbor, ME 04679
207-244-5531
www.hinckleyyachts.com
Builders of classic yachts

**The Maine Coast Boathouse**
1275 Atlantic Highway
Northport, ME 04849
207-338-0100

**Robert H. Perry Yacht Designers**
5801 Phinney Avenue North
Suite 100
Seattle, WA 98103
206-789-7212
www.perryboat.com
Custom yacht designers

**Sparkman & Stephens**
529 Fifth Avenue
14th floor
New York, NY 10017
212-661-1240 (Design)
www.sparkmanstephens.com
Naval architecture, marine engineering,
yacht and charter brokers, marine
insurance

There are many points on the compass rose. I had to locate the few that were meant for me and head for those that summoned me with a passion, for they were the ones that gave meaning to my life.

—Richard Bode

# nautical reading

## books

### FICTION

Barrett, Andrea. **Servants of the Map: Stories.** New York: W.W. Norton & Company, 1996.

——. **Ship Fever.** New York: W.W. Norton & Company, 1996.

——. **The Voyage of Narwhal.** New York: W.W. Norton & Company, 1999.

Coleridge, Samuel Taylor. **Rime of the Ancient Mariner.** New York: Dover Publications, 1970.

DeFoe, Daniel. **Robinson Crusoe.** New York: Princeton Review, 2001.

Forester, C. S. **The Horatio Hornblower Series.** Boston: Little Brown & Co.

Hemingway, Ernest. **The Old Man and The Sea.** New York: Scribner, 1996.

Kipling, Rudyard. **Captains Courageous.** New York: Penguin Putnam—New American Library, 1989.

London, Jack. **The Sea Wolf.** New York: Bantam Classics, 1992.

Melville, Herman. **Moby Dick.** New York: Penguin USA, 2001.

Naslund, Sena Jeter. **Ahab's Wife.** New York: Harper Perennial, 2000.

Nordhoff, Charles. **Mutiny on the Bounty.** London: Little, Brown & Co., 1989.

Ransome, Arthur. **Swallows and Amazons.** Boston: David R. Godine, Inc., 1998.

Sparks, Nicholas. **Message in a Bottle.** New York: Warner Books, 1999.

Woolf, Virginia. **To the Lighthouse.** Philadelphia: Harvest Books, 1990.

### PATRICK O'BRIAN SERIES

**The Aubrey-Maturin Series, 17 Vols.** New York: W.W. Norton & Company, 1997.

**Blue at the Mizzen (Aubrey/Maturin Series).** New York: W.W. Norton & Company, 1999.

**The Commodore (Aubrey-Maturin Series).** New York: W.W. Norton & Company, 1996.

**The Complete Aubrey/Maturin Series 16-Volume Cloth Set** New York: W.W. Norton & Company, 1997.

**Desolation Island.** New York: W.W. Norton & Company, 1991.

**The Fallen.** New York: W.W. Norton & Company, 2002.

**The Far Side of the World.** New York: W.W. Norton & Company, 1992.

**The Fortune of War.** New York: W.W. Norton & Company, 1991.

**The Golden Ocean.** New York: W.W. Norton & Company, 1996.

**H.M.S. Surprise.** New York: W.W. Norton & Company, 1991.

**The Hundred Days (Aubrey/Maturin Series).** New York: W.W. Norton & Company, 1999.

**The Ionian Mission.** New York: W.W. Norton & Company, 1992.

**The Letter of Marque.** New York: W.W. Norton & Company, 1992.

**Master and Commander.** New York: W.W. Norton & Company, 1990.

**The Mauritius Command.** New York: W.W. Norton & Company, 1991.

**Men-of-War: Life in Nelson's Navy.** New York: W.W. Norton & Company, 1995.

**The Nutmeg of Consolation.** New York: W.W. Norton & Company, 1993.

**Post Captain.** New York: W.W. Norton & Company, 1990.

**The Rendezvous and Other Stories.** New York: W.W. Norton & Company, 1994.

**The Reverse of the Medal.** New York: W.W. Norton & Company, 1992.

**The Surgeon's Mate.** New York: W.W. Norton & Company, 1992.

**The Thirteen-Gun Salute.** New York: W.W. Norton & Company, 1992.

**Treason's Harbour.** New York: W.W. Norton & Company, 1992.

**The Truelove.** New York: W.W. Norton & Company, 1993.

**The Unknown Shore.** New York: W.W. Norton & Company, 1996.

**The Wine-Dark Sea.** New York: W.W. Norton & Company, 1994.

**The Yellow Admiral.** New York: W.W. Norton & Company, 1997.

### NONFICTION

Ashley, Clifford W. **The Ashley Book of Knots.** New York: Doubleday, 1993.

Budworth, Geoffrey. **The Complete Book of Decorative Knots: Lanyard Knots, Button Knots, Globe Knots, Turk's Heads, Mats, Hitching, Chains, Plaits.** Guilford, Conn.: The Lyons Press, 1999.

——. **The Ultimate Encyclopedia of Knots and Ropework.** London: Lorenz Books, 1999.

Cordingly, David. **Women Sailors and Sailors' Women: An Untold Maritime History.** New York: Random House, 2001.

Dana, Richard Henry. **Two Years Before the Mast.** Scituate, Mass.: Digital Scanning Inc., 2001.

Fondas, John. **Sailors' Valentines.** New York: Rizzoli, 2002.

Philbrick, Nathaniel. **In the Heart of the Sea: The Tragedy of the Whaleship Essex.** New York: Penguin USA, 2001.

Rousmaniere, John. **America's Cup Book: 1851–1983.** New York: W.W. Norton & Company, 1983.

———. **Fastnet, Force10: The Deadliest Storm in the History of Modern Sailing.** New York: W.W. Norton & Co., 2000.

Smith, Hervey Garrett. **The Marlinspike Sailor.** New York: McGraw-Hill, 1993.

Smith, Robert. **Maritime Museums of North America, Including Canada.** Princeton, N.J.: Finley-Greene Publications, 1998.

Sobel, Dava. **Longitude: The True Story of a Lone Genius Who Solved the Greatest Scientific Problem of His Time.** New York: Walker & Co., 1995.

Tyng, Charles. **Before the Wind: The Memoir of an American Sea Captain 1808–1833.** New York: Penguin, 1999.

PHOTOGRAPHY

Giorgetti, Franco. **The Great Sailing Ships.** New York: Metro Books, 2001.

———. **Sails and Sailing.** Mystic, Conn.: Mystic Seaport Museum Publications, 1999.

Holm, Ed. **Yachting's Golden Age: 1880–1905.** New York: Knopf, 1999.

McBride, Simon. **Under Sail: Aboard the World's Finest Boats.** Muskogee, Okla.: Artisan, 2001.

Rosenfeld, Stanley. **A Century Under Sail.** Mystic, Conn.: Mystic Seaport Museum Publications, 3rd Rep Edition, 2001.

Villiers, Alan. **The Last of the Wind Ships.** New York: W.W. Norton & Company, 2000.

## magazines and periodicals

**The American Neptune**
Peabody Essex Museum
East India Square
Salem, MA 01970
978-745-9500
800-745-4054
www.pem.org
Premium quarterly

**Coastal Living**
2100 Lake Shore Drive
Birmingham, AL 35209
205-877-6000
www.coastalliving.com
Lifestyle magazine

**Marine Art Quarterly**
1657 Post Road
Fairfield, CT 06430
203-259-8753
www.jrusselljinishiangallery
.com/marineartquarterly.htm

**Nautical World Magazine**
www.nauticalworld.com
Boat designers, boatyards, brokers, charters, insurance, marine services, surveyors, transportation, photography

**On The Wind**
Boston Nautical Heritage Group
P.O. Box 379
Stoughton, MA 02072
781-344-1749
www.bostonnautical.com
Bi-weekly e-newsletter

**Sailing**
P.O. Box 249
Port Washington, WI 53074
262-284-3494
www.sailnet.com/sailing

**Sailing World**
P.O. Box 1668
Palm Coast, FL 32142
800-429-0106
www.sailingworld.com

**Sail Magazine**
P.O. Box 56397
Boulder, CO 80323
800-745-7245
www.sailmag.com

**Wooden Boat**
Naskeag Road
P.O. Box 78
Brooklin, ME 04616
207-359-4651
www.woodenboat.com

## websites

www.aboard.co.uk
    Yacht designers website—nautical links, boat finder, market place
www.boat-links.com
www.cr.nps.gov/maritime
www.ils.unc.edu/maritime
www.lighthouse.cc
    Virtual guide to New England lighthouses
www.marinewaypoints.com
www.maritimemuseums.net
    U.S. maritime museums locator
www.nauticaltrivia.com
    Nautical trivia
www.redskyatnight.com
www.sailinglinks.com
www.seacompanion.com
www.smallships.com
    Antique, classic, and tall ship links, museum updates, boat and equipment manufacturers, yacht clubs, charters, cruises and rentals
www.woodenboat.org

## bookstores

**Armchair Sailor Seabooks**
543 Thames Street
Newport, RI 02840
401-847-4252
800-29-CHART
www.seabooks.com
Nautical books, charts, guidebooks, software, and resource books

**The Book & Tackle Shop**
7 Bay Street
Watch Hill, RI 02891
401-596-0700
617-965-0459
Old, rare, new books, postcards

**Crawford's Nautical Books**
Route 33
Tilghman Island, MD 21671
410-886-2418
Books on ships, maritine history, exploration, sailing, yachting

Overhead, the white sails stretched their arms to catch the night wind. They were my sails—my wings—and they had brought me to the sea of my boyhood dreams.

—William Robinson

# bibliography

Baddeley, Jon. **Nautical Antiques and Collectibles.** London: Sotheby's Publications, 1993.

Beavis, Bill, and Richard G. McCloskey. **Salty Dog Talk: The Nautical Origins of Everyday Expressions.** Dobbs Ferry, N.Y.: Sheridan House, 1995.

Brawer, Nicholas A. **British Campaign Furniture: Elegance Under Canvas.** New York: Harry N. Abrams, 2001.

Calasibetta, Charlotte Mankey, Ph.D. **Fairchild's Dictionary of Fashion.** New York: Fairchild Books, 1975, 2000.

Caswell, Christopher, ed. **The Quotable Sailor.** Guilford, Conn.: The Lyons Press, 2001.

Clifford, J. Candace, and Mary Louise Clifford. **Nineteenth-Century Lights: Historic Images of American Lighthouses.** Alexandria, Va.: Cypress Communications, 2000.

———. **Women Who Kept the Lights.** Alexandria, Va.: Cypress Communications, 2000.

Crompton, Samuel Willard. **The Lighthouse Book.** New York: Barnes & Noble Books, 1999.

Cross, Amy Willard. **The Summer House: A Tradition of Leisure.** Toronto: Harper Perennial, 1992.

De Visser, John, and Judy Ross. **At the Water's Edge: Muskoka's Boathouses.** Toronto: Stoddart, 1993.

Doane, Doris. **A Book of Cape Cod Houses.** Boston: David R. Godine, 2000.

German, Andrew W. **Voyages: Stories of America and the Sea.** Mystic, Conn.: Mystic Seaport Museum Publications, 2000.

Glenn, David, and Simon McBride. **Nautical Style: Yacht Interiors and Design.** London: Scriptum Editions, 2000.

Gribbins, Joseph. **Classic Sail.** New York: Friedman/Fairfax, 1998.

Hanson, Hans Jurgen. **Art and the Seafarer: A Historical Survey of the Arts and Crafts of Sailors and Shipwrights.** Translated by James and Inge Moore. New York: Viking Press, 1968.

Herreshoff, Halsey C., ed. **The Sailor's Handbook.** Boston: Little, Brown & Co., 1983.

Hobson, Anthony. **Lanterns That Lit Our World.** Spencertown, N.Y.: Golden Hill Press, 1991, 2000.

Holland, Francis Ross, Jr. **America's Lighthouses: An Illustrated History.** New York: Dover Publications, 1988.

Israel, Fred L., ed. **Lighthouses: Beacons of the Sea: Chronicles from National Geographic.** Philadelphia: Chelsea House Publishers, 2000.

Jeans, Peter D. **An Ocean of Words: A Dictionary of Nautical Words and Phrases.** Seacaucus, N.J.: Birch Lane Press, 1998.

Knox-Johnston, Robin. **Yachting: The History of a Passion.** New York: Hearst Marine Books, 1990.

Lurie, Alison. **The Language of Clothes.** New York: Henry Holt, 1981.

Major, Alan. **Maritime Antiques: An Illustrated Dictionary.** London: The Tantivy Press, 1981.

McQuillan, Deirdre. **The Aran Sweater.** Belfast: Appletree Press, 1993.

Mullins, Lisa C., ed. **New England by the Sea.** Harrisburg, Penn.: The National Historical Society, 1987.

Neill, Peter, ed. **Maritime America: Art and Artifacts from America's Great Nautical Collections.** New York: Balsam Press, 1988.

O'Flynn, Joseph P. **Nautical Dictionary.** Boyne City, Mich.: Harbor House, 1992.

Pastoureau, Michel. **The Devil's Cloth: A History of Stripes & Striped Fabric.** Translated by Jody Gladding. New York: Columbia University Press, 2001.

Pawson, Des. **The Handbook of Knots.** New York: DK Publishing, 1998.

Rhein, Michael J. **Anatomy of the Lighthouse.** New York: Barnes & Noble Books, 2000.

Rogers, John G. **Origins of Sea Terms.** Mystic, Conn.: Mystic Seaport Museum Publications, 1985.

Rosenfeld, Morris and Stanley. **A Century Under Sail.** Mystic, Conn.: Mystic Seaport Museum Publications, 2001.

Schleining, Lon. **Treasure Chests: The Legacy of Extraordinary Boxes.** Newtown, Conn.: Taunton Press, 2001.

Smith, Hervey Garrett. **The Arts of the Sailor: Knotting, Splicing and Ropework.** New York: Dover Publications, 1953, 1990.

Spurr, Daniel. **Yacht Style.** Camden, Me.: International Marine, 1990.

Stilgoe, John R. **Alongshore.** New Haven, Conn.: Yale University Press, 1994.

Tryckare, Tre. **The Lore of Ships.** New York: Crescent Books, 1973.

Volo, Dorothy Denneen, and James M. Volo. **Daily Life in the Age of Sail.** Westport, Conn.: Greenwood Press, 2002.

# acknowledgments

One rainy afternoon in England a couple of years ago, Michael Skott and I sat in a pub when our photo shoot was washed out and talked about new book ideas. Michael, being an avid sailor, wanted to photograph a book on yachting, and I, being passionate about architecture and design, wanted to do a book on New England houses. After many pots of tea and pints of lager, we decided that we could combine our interests and came up with the concept of *Sailing Style.* There is something about the sailing lifestyle that has influenced the little cottages and houses by the sea, and the lighthouses and boathouses nestled in harbors all along the New England coast. We set out to find a vocabulary of building materials, functional designs, and a classic color palette and found it in the places shown in these pages. We also found that the people who love sailing, old wooden boats, and houses by the sea were happy to share their passion with us, take us out on their boats, and introduce us to favorite places, fellow sailors, and a language to communicate "sailing style."

We brought Jill Kirchner Simpson on the team to tell the story and Richard Ferretti to interpret our vision with his designs.

Our appreciation goes to Mystic Seaport for their inspiration, resources, and research that they shared with us.

We'd like to thank Diane and Tom Good and Sue and David White, who sheltered us from the storm of September 11, fed us, sailed us to locations all over Cape Cod, Cuttyhunk, and Martha's Vineyard, and introduced us to quahogs and Dr. and Mrs. Kohn.

We'd also like to thank Steven Mack in Rhode Island for his attention to detail and knowledge of 18th-century New England architecture and nautical design, which inspired us, and Kenneth Martin and Nancy Burden of Maine, whose scholarship on whaling history and private collection of maritime paintings became a part of our story. John Newton spent an afternoon with us explaining bells and chronometers and showing us examples he's collected over the years. To Patrick Gallagher, who led us to the wonderful gatehouse, designed by Hayward Gatch, fitted like a ship's interior; and to Alan Granby and Janice Hyland, who took time out from their busy schedules to let us wander through their amazing maritime library and collection of navigational instruments, we owe our thanks. We also appreciate the help of Rob Kapnek, who took us through the canals and waterways in Bellport Bay to see his favorite lighthouse, and Kirk Roeser, who lives in the lighthouse and let us photograph it.

To all our old friends who took care of us on our travels: Kathy Hay and George Davis welcomed us to Nantucket; Mallory Marshall introduced us to Mark Umbach and John Lyle in Maine; and Kevin Jacobs reminded me that Bob Smith had the best little house and mother in Cuttyhunk. We appreciate the help of Charlotte Johnson, who welcomed us back to the Rose Island Lighthouse, where I had spent a memorable time many years ago; Keith Scott Morton and Chris Churchill, who hosted us at the perfect seaside cottage in Orient; and Ellen O'Neill, who opened the doors of her perfect blue-and-white striped house in Sag Harbor.

We were also able to stay on course with our story with the help of Roy Hardin, Claudia and Geoff Broderick, and Ann Kim, our on-site crew.

A big thank-you to Liv Blumer for all her support and encouragement and to all those at Clarkson Potter for helping to make this happen, especially Lauren Shakely, whose vision kept us on course, Marysarah Quinn and Jane Treuhaft, who art directed us along the way, and Mark McCauslin and Joan Denman, who kept us shipshape all the way into port.

# index